Adoption Healing

a path to recovery

Supplement

Joe Soll 조살, LCSW-R, DAPA

Please direct all correspondence to:
Joe Soll, LCSW
74 Lakewood Drive
Congers, NY 10920
Email: joesoll@adoptionhealing.com

"Adoption Healing ... a path to recovery - Supplement," by Joe Soll, LCSW, DAPA.. ISBN 978-0-615-51370-6.

Library of Congress Control Number: 2012905129.

Manufactured in the United States of America.

Also by Joe Soll

Adoption Healing... a path to recovery (for adoptees) 2000

with Karen Wilson Buterbaugh as co-author,
Adoption Healing (For women who lost children to adoption) 2003

with Lori Paris as co-author,
Evil Exchange 2007, *Fatal Flight* 2010

Dedication

To my natural mother,
whoever and wherever she is,
with love,
and to all those who either are or were
Missing In Adoption

Contents

Author's Notes xi

Acknowledgments xv

Preface xvii

Proceed Gently xix

Doomed xxi

Introduction 1

Part One: Missing from previous Adoption Healing books 7

Chapter 00: Unlovable.....................................19
Chapter 0: PTSD...20
Chapter 1: I Feel Like a Hotdog 29
Chapter 2: Affirmations the Easy Way.....................33
Chapter 3: Kaboom..36
Chapter 4: Baloney! 42
Chapter 5: Walls 48
Chapter 6: When Your Inner Child Doesn't Talk 52
Chapter 7: Preparation for Search: Why?..................55
Chapter 8: The "R" Word 59
Chapter 9: Special Chosen and Lucky.....................63
Chapter 10: Fear of Mommy Love 66
Chapter 11: Conflict of Two Moms 70
Chapter 12: Her Absence Filled My World..................74
Chapter 13: Searching 78
Chapter 14: Genetic Attraction...........................81
Chapter 15: Who Said That?...............................84

Chapter 16: Good Grief 89
Chapter 17: Graves 92
Chapter 18: Taking Charge of Your Life 98
Chapter 19: Fitting In 110

Part Two: Appendices **114**

Appendix A: The Respect We Never Got 115
Appendix B: Loss in the Adoption Handoff 122
Appendix C: Adoptee's Preparation for Search 126
Appendix D: Mother's Preparation for Search 130
Appendix E: Guidelines for Reunion 134
Appendix F: Healing Weekends 137
Appendix G: How to Love Your Inner Child 139
Appendix H: Chat Room 142
Appendix I: A, B, C's of Searching 145
Appendix J: Search Resources 150
Appendix K: Resources and Readings 151
Appendix L: Charter of Adoptee Rights 155
Appendix M: Myths & Facts 158
Appendix N: Personal Bill of Rights 165
Appendix O: U.N. Convention on the Rights of the Child 167

Epilogue 169

About the Author 173

My Books 175

Author's Notes

"The horrors of war pale beside the loss of a mother" - Anna Freud   "or child"- JS

A few summers ago, I attended a barbecue given by a friend of mine at his home in upstate New York. At one point I went inside his home and as I was passing through the living room, I saw a book lying on a coffee table. "The Complete Idiot's Guide to Zen Living." Knowing nothing about Zen, I picked it up and opened to a page at random. The page I turned to was the beginning of a section entitled, **When Bad Things Happen.** I read a few pages and knew I had to buy the book.

I went outside and enjoyed the barbecue but my unconscious mind was hard at work, processing what I had read. When I got home, I ordered the Zen book and when it arrived a few days later, I immersed myself in it. The more I read, the more I realized that I had unknowingly been applying some Zen principles in my work and in my own life. I picked up the text that I use for visualizations at the Adoption Healing weekends and saw that the entire book, "What We May Be" is based on Zen thinking. I continued to study and apply the principles more and more in my everyday life. The Zen work I am talking about is about the way we think, not about religion. I hope I have piqued your interest enough for you to explore Zen thinking. This has changed my life. I hope you will let it change yours.

Much of the work in the original "Adoption Healing... a path to recovery" is based on Zen thinking, even though I was unaware of it when I wrote it. I wished I had known more about Zen so I could have included more of the principles in the book. This revelation led me to think about the things I have learned and come to understand better in the eleven years since my first book was published and decided to write this book.

Some things bear repeating and, of necessity, parts of this book that were in the original Adoption Healing are included in this work. And, of necessity, some of the things in this book will be repeated to drive the information home. I hope that what is presented here will facilitate your understanding of the adoption healing process. I've worked with almost as many natural mothers[1] as adoptees and it is clear to me that the psychological experiences of the adoptee and the natural mother when they are separated are almost identical. The aftermath, the effects of their experience on their lives, runs a parallel course for both adoptees and natural mothers. I also believe that the experience of the separation is the same for both, happening at the same time on a cellular level.

The natural mother experience has, for the most part, been unheard, unacknowledged by society, yet the effects of the loss of their babies is life-long and profound, and needs to be understood as well.

My hope is that this work will provide a method of healing for both adoptees and natural mothers and provide to all those touched by adoption an understanding of the profound wounds inflicted by the separation of mother and child. We need to have empathy for what happened to all those affected by adoption loss and to do that, I believe that every adoptee and every mother of adoption loss needs to read about and understand the psychological trauma of adoption separation and its aftermath for all who endured it.

---

[1] The term "natural mother" is used to describe a woman who has lost her child to adoption, not a woman who is pregnant.

As you read this book, no matter what your life experience has been, you may well become emotionally stimulated and have feelings of anxiety, pain and sadness. Please know that this is normal and that you are not alone in your feelings. In the United States, referring only to non-kinship adoption, there are eight million adoptees, sixteen million natural parents and sixteen million adoptive parents; forty million people intimately involved in every adoption.

Finally, for convenience, I have chosen to use feminine pronouns throughout the book. There are an equal number of men involved in adoption and it is not my intent to exclude them by my use of the feminine pronouns. Also for convenience, I use the term adoptive parents to include prospective adoptive parents as well as those parents who have already adopted a child. It should be noted that the loss of a father by the adoptee and the loss experienced by a father are both serious and need to be dealt with but are beyond the scope of this book.

Before we go further, I suggest you get a notebook or diary, etc. so you can journal your thoughts and feelings as we go on this journey together.

Acknowledgments

"I know now that this healing happens in spirals and
layers and NOT in steps like a ladder." SARK

I would like to thank the many individuals without whom this book would not have been written: Mary Sussillo, whose infinite patience finally allowed me to lower my walls and deal with my feelings. Diana who has remained a constant light in my life for almost five decades. Darlene Gerow for her contribution of "Loss in the Adoption Handoff" and the cover design, and Lisa Goldberg and Celeste for their editing of my book.

Bob Andersen, Clarissa Pinkola Estés, the late Betty Jean Lifton, Rickie Solinger, and Nancy Verrier for their friendship, support and wisdom.

Within the adoption reform movement, Florence Fisher who showed me the way in the beginning; Rickie Solinger & Nancy Verrier, for the contribution of energy, knowledge and healing that they gave at so many of my conferences; Don Humphrey and the Honorable Mary Smith for their tenacious fight for my right to my heritage; the late Jean Paton, the first adoptee with the courage to search and write about it a half century ago; Carol Chandler for just being there, and finally to Julie Goldman who stood by me through thick and thicker in my struggle to accomplish my goals.

For their dedication to adoption reform, my special "March Family" who shared with me the six yearly walks from New York City to Washington, D.C., trekking down 250 miles of highway together in 100 degree heat, rain and exhaust fumes, in an effort to make the world a better place for those touched by adoption.

For composing the beautiful song, *I Wonder Who My Mother Is?* for me to sing and record, I am grateful to the prolific and incomparable American song-writer, the late Gladys Shelley.

Alexsandra, Marnie and Nickie, my foreign correspondents and supporters. Susan Hawvermale for her friendship and validating childhood truths that no one else could ever or would ever verify.

The Korean community for taking me at face value, accepting me and helping me learn the language.

Finally, my clients, group members, chatters and retreaters from whom I have learned more than any school could ever teach.

Preface

"They always say time changes
things, but you actually have to
change them yourself." – Andy Warhol

As I lecture around the country, in book stores, libraries, social service agencies and other facilities, I am often told, usually angrily, by one or more of the attendees that I have broken their bubble, destroyed their dream.

"What bubble have I broken or dream destroyed?" I ask.

"That my child will be happy and have no pain. I didn't want to know what you have told me and I don't want it to be so!"

This book is about the realities of adoption and the realities of the inner world of those separated by adoption. I hope this book will help all those affected by adoption better understand the realities as opposed to the myths.

Much of what I write I have learned from the vast knowledge and wisdom of my mentors and colleagues. Also, a great deal of what I write comes from 28 years of empirical research, working with adopted children, adolescents and adults, natural parents and adoptive parents.

I am not happy about what I have written here, but it needed to be written. It needs to be recognized as knowledge that can help heal those already hurt and help prevent some of the hurt for those who may become involved in or impacted by adoption. I am writing this book as an adoptee talking from the heart to his millions of adopted "brothers and sisters," as a son to millions of his natural parents and adoptive parents and as a colleague to his fellow mental health professionals.

I hope this gift can be accepted and ultimately unwrapped for use.

JS, Congers, NY
October, 2011

Proceed Gently

"And the day came when the risk to remain closed in a bud became more painful than the risk it took to blossom." ~Anais Nin

In the following pages, I will offer exercises, visualizations and affirmations. *If you are currently in therapy, please get your therapist's approval before starting these exercises, visualizations and affirmations.* You *can* do it by yourself using your adult self as a wise and caring person, but you still need your therapist's approval. In some of the exercises, your adult self will nurture your wounded inner child. You can do the exercises alone, but it would be better, at least in the beginning, for you to do them with a nurturing and supportive friend or even better with a support group.

The information, exercises, visualizations and inner child work in this book are not meant to be a substitute for psychotherapy or any other healing work you are doing. The work of this book is highly charged in many ways. Go slow and be patient with yourself. This work takes time. If you start to feel like it's too much, STOP. Put down the book, take some deep breaths and say the word "Relax" out loud in your head. If you still feel unsafe, reach out to a friend, relative, sponsor or therapist.

Doomed

Again and again, I hear adoptees and moms tell me they think they are doomed or jinxed.

"... Once you're born, you can't go back,
or change your stars of zodiac:
Your horoscope
leaves not much hope
if you're open'd up to stayin' jinxed!

       And yet if you can swing it,
       You can wing it,
       Just buyin' time...
       And then before you snap,
       You'll break that trap,
       You'll start in to climb!

Tho' the Devil fool ya,
You can make with Hallelujah,
And a great big Yes.
Don't try to guess.
Why your blessings seem to be mixed.
If you have endurance,
You can win,
Cause not to have endurance,
Is mortal sin - -
So find the key, the open door,
And never, never, nevermore be jinxed!" - Bone & Fenton

Take the above to heart! I did!

Introduction

"Your mother loved you so much that she gave you away."

"If you really love your baby you will give her up for adoption."

Those two sentences refer to the genesis of adoption trauma. Bear with me.

In the summer of 1979, while standing on the top of the north tower of the World Trade Center, supervising the installation of the WOR-TV television antenna on the broadcast tower, (Yes, this is what I did for twenty years; design and build radio and television transmission facilities) I heard a loud noise and looked south where I could see a Delta Airlines 1011 Jet descending through the cloud cover. Along with the dozens of workmen and engineers who were there that day, I flattened myself on the roof in terror. I was sure the jet was going to hit the building. Being on the flight path to LaGuardia airport, it was common for jets to travel above us but this time the jet was only a few hundred feet above us and we all panicked.

Why am I saying this? I started my engineering career in 1963 in the Empire State Building. I was there... either inside the building supervising transmitter installations or in the TV tower on the top of the building. Every day I was afraid, on some level, that a plane would hit the building and knock it over. After all, it had been hit in 1945 by a military plane that was lost in the fog and the Empire State Building was also on the flight path to LaGuardia. I did my work by being numb. I was numb to adoption and numb to my perceived danger working on these tall buildings. While being on top of the Empire State Building or the World Trade Center one could always feel the buildings swaying, which they were both designed to do. This continuous movement increased my fears. Especially in a storm, it seemed like the building would fall over which added to my general inner turmoil.

On 9/11, watching television in tears as the World Trade Center crumbled, I became terrified. I was in a state of panic. My worst "conscious" fears had come true. My worst unconscious fear was of being abandoned but I was unaware of this. I sat on the couch, sobbing, terrified but truly unaware of the real underpinnings of my panic... the separation from my mother at birth. My original trauma.

I cancelled the regular Wednesday adoption support group meeting for the next day, the first cancellation of a meeting, at that time, in over 14 years. The city was asking commuters to stay away, so my traveling was not possible and I was greatly relieved. I gave great thought psychologically, as to how I was going to manage going in to the city. I, along with most of the residents of the NY metro area, was petrified that there would be another attack.

The following Wednesday, I drove in and parked my car. As I walked out of the garage, I looked up and saw a plane smash into a tall apartment building. I closed my eyes and leaned against the building. I looked up again. No plane. As I walked to my office the same thing happened again and again. Every time I looked up I saw a plane smash into a building and then a fiery explosion.

PTSD - Post traumatic Stress Disorder is the result of trauma that is untreated. The separation of mother and child (the reason does not matter) is a trauma of the highest order. PTSD is very treatable with proper help, so do not despair. A large portion of this book is devoted to healing from the adoption related traumas that cause PTSD.

I had trouble eating and sleeping. I was functioning only by keeping very, very busy. The local stations were reporting that free therapy for PTSD was being offered to all those in New York City who were having problems. I called and three therapists were sent to my office to see me at a mutually conducive time.

The following week, as soon as they came in, sat and introduced themselves, I started to sob. They were Very, Very Good. They asked me right away if I had had any other traumas in my life. "Yes, I'm adopted and I lost my mother at birth," was my reply.

"So 9/11 woke up your previous trauma as it did for anyone who had suffered from a trauma previously," was their response. They saw the connection immediately.

We talked, I cried about 9/11 and I cried about losing my mom. They helped me understand in a new way how insidious PTSD really is. I knew I suffered from it adoption wise but had never seen it in action from the onset as I did following 9/11.

The three therapists guided me through what I help my clients do, understand that even though it seems like it, the trauma cannot repeat. 9/11 cannot happen again. Other terrorism, yes. Other losses of sacred relationships, yes. But the traumas we have had cannot repeat and we need to do good self-talk (inner child work) to get past the minute by minute, hour by hour, day by day terror. I needed three sessions with the therapists to get past my terror but my visions of plane crashes into buildings stopped immediately. I do not walk around worrying about repeat terrorism in any way that interferes with my life. We all know that we are at risk, but we can stop worrying about it in a disruptive way.

I had stopped fearing "abandonment" long ago with the help of my therapist and my own inner child work. This experience helped me help my clients even more since I had a present day experience of seeing the genesis of PTSD.

The original Adoption Healing came off the presses in September 2000 and a year later the tragedy struck. Had my book been written after 9/11 it would have been somewhat different due to my conscious trauma of that sad day.

Imagine what it's like to hearing those two sentences at the beginning of this chapter. And then being given no comfort. For sixteen million adoptees and natural mothers in the U.S. alone those words forebode a pervasive and *fiercely debilitating* aftermath of adoption. Their long-term impact is an existential catch-22 in which adoptees and mothers of adoption loss are forced to choose between the socially unacceptable reality they experience and a distorted, but socially sanctioned, interpretation of their reality as determined by others.

Based on over twenty eight years of daily empirical research with literally thousands of adoptees, (children, adolescents and adults) and mothers of adoption loss and others separated by adoption, this supplement to *Adoption Healing* sheds new light on ways to heal from the crippling effect of these traumatic events. The ideas and theories expressed in this book are the result of the research, extensive readings, seminars and conversations with other adoption educators/mental health professionals.

From infancy, adoptees are bombarded by verbal and non-verbal messages from the outer world that directly negate and contradict their inner feelings and experiences. They are expected to be happy on their birthday, often the anniversary of their separation from their natural mother. Adoptees are told that their natural mother loved them so much that she gave them away – a statement that must certainly leave them wondering about the desirability of being loved, to say nothing of the motives of their mother. They are given to understand both that their real mother gave them away and that their adoptive mother is their real mother. Most damaging of all, adoptees are assured by the rest of us that they feel no sense of loss, no rage at having been abandoned.

Mothers of adoption loss are expected to forget that they had a child and to go on "as if" they did not give birth. Adoptees get a substitute mother. Mothers of adoption loss are left with full

> "Wow, there really was a woman who gave birth to me!" Marc, adoptee, age 37, upon learning the name of his natural mother.

breasts, raging hormones and unmanageable pain. Each has suffered a psychological death with no way to mourn.

Caught between these conflicting messages, adoptees and mothers of adoption loss are stuck in an emotional limbo, unable to accept either their inner, private reality or the fictional reality presented by those around them. Instead of an integrated whole, their sense of self splinters, or *fractures,* into separate pieces. Since adoptees and mothers of adoption loss must function in the outer world if they are to survive, their inner world can become increasingly repressed, eventually slipping out of reach. Survival is purchased at a heavy price, however, for without access to their inner feelings, people are unable to live authentic lives.

This supplement to *Adoption Healing* has been written in an attempt to provide adoptees, adoptive parents, and natural parents with additional knowledge and tools that can be used in healing this *fracture.* Vignettes and quotes are presented throughout the book to illustrate the real-life manifestations of adoption-related problems, and the successful growth and healing possible when these issues are understood and tackled correctly.

Adoption is a family issue; thus, its effects extend far beyond the realm of adoptee, adoptive parents and natural parents. For this reason, *Adoption Healing* has much to offer the many others – siblings, spouses, grandparents, and children of adoptees – who are also struggling to cope with the impact of adoption.

This book is intended for both professional psychotherapists and the general public. While it would not be possible to bridge these two audiences in writing about most subjects, the nascent field of adoption psychology is an exception in that professional and lay groups overlap. Unlike other areas of psychology, in which professionals have led the way, the thinking expressed in this book has been generated to a significant degree by the

> "Though her soul requires seeing, the culture around her requires sightlessness. Though her soul wishes to speak its truth, she is pressured to be silent. Neither the child's soul nor her psyche can accommodate this." – *Women Who Run With the Wolves* – Clarissa Pinkola Estés

efforts of adoptees and natural mothers to understand and define their own experience. Arising in large part from the grassroots search/reunion movement, the field of adoption psychology is therefore unique in the degree to which lay people have contributed to the development of psychological theory. In recognition of this, *Adoption Healing* is directed to all the "therapists" in adoptees' lives – professional counselors, adoptive parents, natural parents, spouses and family members, and finally, adoptees themselves

This book is an attempt to educate, and an attempt to understand one of the most misunderstood subjects in the world. This book is not about finger pointing. It *is* about learning from our mistakes so that we can perhaps reduce suffering in the future, especially for those who are separated from their children and their mothers and their other family members.

Part One

Missing from Adoption Healing 1 & 2

Injuries caused by separation of mother and child can, in time and with work, be dealt with effectively to the point where the loss will not interfere daily in our lives. Instead, the pain might rear its head a few times a year. We may need to cry--get a hug and perhaps vent our anger--but the pain will pass more quickly each time.

For this book to be helpful to you, I suggest that you need to have read "Primal Wound" and one or both of my books, "Adoption Healing... a path to recovery" and understand the concepts laid out in them.

"I don't know what I don't know" - anon

"Sometimes I think the 9 months I spent inside my mom was the best time of my life and the happiest and most content and whole and complete I've ever been." - anon

Last minute thoughts:

Strength

Do you know where you got the strength to do this work? I used to think that we got stronger by facing adversity. I was mistaken. Either you are born with the strength or you are not. It may take time to find it, to be able to use it but it's genetic. We have it from birth and we need to be proud that we have found our strength and are able to use it. Our looks, our talents, our brains come from our natural families. Our temperament is highly, genetically predisposed, and so are our tastes in food, and hobbies and much, much more. We can learn to cherish what we have that helps us heal. We may not find our strength until we are in our 40's or 50's or even 60's, and that is not a sign of any kind of weakness. Each of us has our own timetable for healing. Each of us does it on time for us. I believe that most people do not have the strength to do this... You are reading this book, so you do!

Alarms

People often complain to me that they wish they did not feel their emotions. They express anger at being angry or sad, etc.

Cars have alarms to tell us a door is open, seat belt is not fastened, we are low on gas, etc. Airplanes have alarms to tell the pilot he is too low, he is low on fuel, a cargo door is not latched, etc. Our homes have alarms to warn us of CO_2 and to warn us of fire and smoke.

Our bodies have alarm systems too. We get a fever warning us of the flu, perhaps, or a tummy ache warning us of too much acid.

Our emotions warn us of problems within our psyche. Without our emotions we could literally be dead. For example, anger gets our adrenalin flowing in times of danger. Without it, we could perish in a dangerous situation by not reacting. Sadness means we need to cry and let out pain and the toxic chemicals that exist within tears. Remorse may help us understand things we did that we do not want to repeat. If we don't pay attention to our emotions we will likely pay a heavy price indeed. Our physical and mental health will likely be harmed in serious ways.

Many of us, myself included, existed for years in a state of numbness, hiding from pain to survive. To truly live, we must find a way to feel all of our emotions. We can do this by respecting our fears, but trying little by little to feel our own emotions. We can learn, by experience and with the support of others, that our emotions will not hurt us but in fact will help us to experience life fully.

Please pay attention to your personal alarms!

Little by little you can come alive. Little by little you can thrive.

Words

The words we use affect our unconscious mind, even if consciously they have no impact. E.g. Repeatedly tell a child that she is stupid and eventually she will act that way. Even the words we say to ourselves will have a profound effect on our lives. There are many examples of this throughout the book. Negative thinking, negative expectations, often have negative repercussions.

Fear of Fear

Some things are so terrifying to think about that we are not aware of the terror on a conscious level. If we acknowledge being afraid or terrified of something, then we will have to get in touch with that terror itself and when that is intolerable we lose our awareness. This is Fear of Fear and is a common occurrence for trauma victims.

Committees

Every person has an inner child for every age they ever were. For the purposes of this book, adoptees should be talking to their inner child who is between the ages of 6-1/2 to 8 years old. Mothers of adoption loss should be talking to their inner child, their younger self who just lost her child to adoption. At times one or more older ICs may well just show up and if that happens, imagine your ICs sitting with you in a safe place, perhaps your living room.

Consider them your "committee" and talk to them in a loving and nurturing way. Our ICs are always watching and listening to everything that goes on so talking to them as a committee can be very helpful. They all need to know they are safe at all times. That what is happening to *you* is not happening to them. This fact, that the committee is always watching and listening, is what can trigger a panic attack... something in today's world reminds them of the past trauma and they think it *is* happening again.

Wrist Rubbing

One of the things a mother does to calm a crying baby is to gently caress the back of her wrist. Since adoptees were part of their mother's bodies, adoptees and their moms share the same skin. It can be very comforting for an adoptee in pain to close her eyes and very gently rub the back of a wrist with the fingers of the other hand, imagining it is her mom doing it. A mom may get comfort by closing her eyes and gently rubbing her wrist and imagining she is comforting her lost child.

Crying

Many of us have been told that crying is for sissies or crybabies or weaklings, etc. We have been told to be strong and not cry. Food for thought: Crying hurts, yes? So, if crying hurts and I let myself do it, then must I not *be* strong to let it happen? Perhaps those who tell us not to cry are the weak ones, afraid of their own feelings? Think about it!

Un-American!

An A & E documentary once referred to me as an "Adoption Terrorist" because of my efforts to educate. Adoption in the United States is almost a social imperative. Google and read, "When Infertility Goes Shopping" on line. Mainstream America sees adoption is seen as a win-win for everyone. Many countries have virtually eliminated adoption from within their shores and here in the U.S., people brag about it. In my efforts to educate, I approached the dean of my graduate school and suggested that I or someone else teach courses on adoption and foster care issues. To my dismay, after much hemming and hawing, she told me that the school could not, under any circumstances, teach adoption issues because... it would mean there was something wrong with adoption and that would antagonize the many trustees who were adoptive parents and that would hurt the school financially. I was appalled. I hope you are appalled enough to write letters to your local institutions of higher learning and press the issue.

Hollywood

I've often heard adoptees say, "I am in the wrong movie." I was taken out of my natural role of being with my own family and placed and placed in a movie with strangers. I do not know my lines, I am not allowed to know the beginning of the movie and I have to ad lib my life. Moms are in the wrong movie too, deprived of being able to raise their child, being in limbo, not being able to be themselves. By doing our healing work, we can reclaim ourselves. We cannot go back and fix the past but we can become the producers and directors of our movies and live authentic lives.

Fog

> "An infant has no way to adapt to the sudden disappearance of it's mother/self, especially when she has just entered a world which no longer includes the safety of her mother's womb. Anyone except this original mother, whose rhythms and resonance the infant knows and is in tune with, is foreign and dangerous." - Nancy Verrier, **Coming Home to Self**

Our unconscious mind has some mechanisms to protect or defend us against the emotional pain of severe trauma. One of these defense mechanisms is repression. Repression buries memories, feelings and thoughts without our conscious knowledge. Once an event and all the memories/feelings/thoughts associated with it is repressed, we do not consciously know it ever existed. However all the repressed memories etc., affect our daily lives. Meanwhile we go around in what I've heard described as being in fog. We are numb in many ways so we do not see clearly. We are looking through glasses that are tinted by the fog of our trauma.

Consider what it's like if you were born without sight and then one day, a miracle. You are given the gift of sight. You open your eyes and for the first time you see something. Bright light! This is very painful, like coming into the sunlight after being in a movie house for a few hours. After you get used to the brightness and the pain subsides, you have to learn how to live in this new world of sight. You have to learn what each object is. Oh, that is a bird. That is the sky. That color is blue. It takes a long time to learn what the millions of never-before seen images are and how they are now part of your existence, your life experience.

Coming out of the fog means learning what the previously hidden memories/thoughts/emotions are and how they are now part of your existence, your life experience. Coming out of the fog, which is necessary for healing and living an authentic life filled with joy instead of being numb, is painful and terrifying... in the beginning. The rewards will become self-evident. Enjoy!

It's personal!

We adoptees and moms tend to take things personally. The things that have happened to us are not because of us or who we are as people. Our adoption trauma is due to society and its thoughts and subsequent rules about women, sexual activity and pregnancy. When we can own this concept our feelings will change as well and we will not hurt the way we do. We can learn to control what we think and therefore have control over our suffering. When we stop taking things personally, we have a freedom we did not have before.

"Orphan babies don't cry. They learn there's no point in it." – Anon

"Without knowing one's forbears for two generations one cannot have a sense of actuality. Actuality is feeling that that you and your life are real." – Erik Erikson as reported by Robert J. Lifton

> **EER**   Doing our work can be so intense that we need an **E**motional **E**mergency **R**oom. A safe place to express our feelings, knowing that they will not be dismissed or invalidated. A place where we will be respected and protected. When one is in intense pain, one tends to be self-centered. This is understandable. People in an **EER** deserve *tender loving care*. Just make sure you get it.. Get help, good help. Join an adoption support group... face-to-face is best, on line is next best and a chat room can also be very helpful. Read and read some more. Find an adoption savvy therapist. In my mind they need to be willing to read or have read, *Primal Wound* and believe in its principles to be able to help. Find a safe way to let your pain out, and, as often as possible with "enlightened or loving witnesses", those who have had a similar experience. No matter what, do not give up. One guarantee… If you give up, you stay in pain. If you do this work, you will heal.

Love relationships

Sadly, relationship difficulties are very common for adoptees and natural moms.

My basic beliefs as to what we must do to be able to have healthy love relationships:

1. We must know we were and are lovable.
2. We must grieve the loss of our primal relationship as a mom ora baby with our other.
3. We must stop being afraid of being loved.
4. We must stop being afraid of being left.
5. We must stop thinking that a love relationship will fix our problems.
6. We must stop trying to get back what we lost.
7. We must stop believing that being loved will make us happy.
8. We must nurture our IC daily.
9. We must accept the different-ness of our other.
10. We must find acceptance of our journey

Assumptions!

We adoptees and moms also tend to make assumptions that keep us in pain. We very often do this without proof or facts. So the question is, if we have no proof or facts, why make up bad assumptions? Why not create good assumptions.

Example #1: If I have no knowledge of why I was not kept, why not presume that my mother was not allowed to keep me instead of presuming she did not care about me? (This causes great anguish.)

Example #2: If my child is being standoffish, why not presume that she is afraid of her feelings, instead of presuming she does not love me or care about me? (The latter causing great anguish)

The old saying has validity: If I **AssUme**, I make an Ass out of You and Me.

Choices!

Why do we often have such a hard time making choices, even what we wish to have to eat?

1: Lack of entitlement: We had no choice at the beginning. (The beginning being birth and separation.)

2: We don't know what we feel, so how can we possibly know what we want to do if our feelings are hidden?

3: We are afraid to choose wrong for fear of possible repercussions.

4: As adoptees, we were chosen, so we tend wait for things/people to choose us.

5. We don't want to live with guilt if we've made the wrong decision. (And for adoptees, if we make a decision like an adult, then we are responsible for the consequences. It's easier to remain a child and not be responsible for anything.)

ERC

I look at the work we need to do as **E**motional **R**oot **C**anal.

Just as I cannot imagine a dentist doing his own root canal, I cannot imagine an adoptee or mom doing their own healing. We need to do our work with enlightened or loving others. Face-to-Face in a support group is best, private therapy with someone knowledgeable in adoption issues plus treatment of PTSD and grief work would also be a very good idea. Include reading as much adoption literature as possible along with journaling and channeling anger.

> "Inner child work is essential. It's the essence of growth as a whole person" - Cheryl Richardson

Dental root canal will save a tooth but it creates a dead tooth. Our ERC work will open up our hidden feelings, allowing us to grieve and ultimately to experience life fully instead of just existing.

Inner Child Work

Everyone in the world does Inner Child work without even being aware of it. Everyone talks to themselves out loud in their head, having conversations with themselves and with others. Doing that is Inner Child work. Inner Child work is inner dialogue done consciously with the older adult self teaching and reassuring the younger, inner self (child).

> Personally, I do inner child work every single day. It keeps me balanced. I hope you will do it daily too.

Preparation for Inner Child Work

This may sound silly but humor me!

Close your eyes, say the word "Relax" out loud in your head. Visualize yourself in some place that you'd like to be to get away from it all, some place safe for just you. Perhaps the beach, a cabin in the woods, a lakefront camping site. I want you to let yourself be there. Not see yourself there but be there so much so that you might:

Smell salt air or the air of a pine forest
Hear water gurgling or the sound of leaves rustling in the breeze.
Feel the sun on your body or the breeze on your face.
See waves breaking on the shore or birds flying by.

If you are having a hard time with this, try to visualize someone you feel safe with, a good friend perhaps, and let yourself be in their home for dinner, for example, and just be there as part of the action. Don't see yourself eating dinner, be there eating dinner.
Be there. Say the word "Relax" out loud in your head again. This might take time to do but it's very important to be able to just be there, not see yourself but be yourself… there in that safe place.

As I said earlier, for the purposes of this book, adoptees should be talking to their inner child who is between the ages of 6-1/2 to 8 years old, in a nurturing and loving way[2]. Mothers of adoption loss should

---

[2] The age of cognition. For our inner child work to be effective, adoptees need to talk to their IC of that age.

16

be talking to their inner child, their younger self who just lost her child to adoption in a nurturing and loving way.

Next, imagine that your younger self is there in this safe place. You will both be there. Walk up to younger you, look younger you in the eyes and say, "Hi, I am you when you are all grown up and I've come back to help you!"

If you are having difficulty finding younger you in this safe place then... Adoptees, look for her in the home you were in at her age. Perhaps in her bedroom. Go there first, then walk thru the house calling her name. She'll be there. Moms, try your hospital room, just after your baby was taken, or wherever you went after the hospital. Be patient. She is waiting for you to show up!

Imagine that younger you, your IC, is like someone you come upon in a mall or an airport, lost, alone, afraid, wanting her mommy. It may take her time to feel safe enough to talk. Be patient with her. Be patient with yourself. I presume you did not take Inner Child work 101 in school so this is probably new for you. It is a process and process means taking time to occur.

Go to her several times a day, say hello and tell her you love her and that she is safe. Eventually, she will start to talk to you.

One more thing:

Before you do something, THINK and be sure you are...

Thoughtful
Honest
Intelligent
Necessary
Kind

One very last thing. Two days ago I was on the phone with someone from the utility company talking about my bill. He was being rather dense. While I was trying to figure out how to communicate better with him, I heard my IC say, "He's a googlehead!" Well, I don't talk this way and I never heard the word googlehead before, nor do I know what it means. My inner child was listening and made up this word for the person to whom I was talking. This is proof that our ICs are listening to everything we say or do. I think my IC was right to call that guy a googlehead!

Let us begin!

> "His older self had taught his younger self a language which the older self knew because the younger self, after being taught, grew up to be the older self and was, therefore, capable of teaching." - Robert A. Heinlein

Chapter 00

Things That Make A Baby Unlovable

Chapter 0

Post Traumatic Stress Disorder

"Adoption Loss is the only trauma in the world where the victims are expected by the whole of society to be grateful" - The Reverend Keith C. Griffith, MBE

Post-traumatic stress disorder (PTSD) is a serious mental condition. You can get PTSD after living through or seeing a traumatic event, such as war, a hurricane, rape, physical abuse or a bad accident. PTSD makes you feel extremely stressed and terrified after the danger is over. It affects your life and the people around you.

PTSD victims re-experience the event again and again in several ways. They may have frightening dreams and memories of the event, think they are going through the experience again (flashbacks that seem to be in the now), or become upset during anniversaries of the event.

Labeling PTSD victims as ill or diseased or crazy makes it harder to treat so, as I was taught in shrink school. I prefer no labeling but we must recognize that those separated by adoption do suffer a trauma and have PTSD unless they are given help. In my opinion therefore, victims of PTSD are not mentally ill, but rather have normal reactions to very abnormal situations that leave the victim unable to function in important areas of life. These difficulties in functioning are fixable.

Being lied to can also cause PTSD. Being told your parents died in a car-crash (as thousands of adoptees were told) can easily cause PTSD. Being told your baby died in childbirth (as thousands of moms were told) can easily cause PTSD as well.

Most important of all, the loss of a mother or baby to adoption is a trauma and unless treated causes PTSD. The symptoms may not be obvious but the trauma is there and needs to be addressed.

Here are some lies created by the unconscious mind that I've heard from moms and adoptees. Lies created to hide from pain...

I'm not angry
I'm glad I was adopted
Adoption is not an issue.
Being adopted does not bother me
Why would I want to search for her, she didn't want me?
She is not my mother
I have parents who wanted me
I didn't want my baby
Losing my baby did not cause me pain
Why would I search for my baby? She has a good life.
She is not really my child
I am not a mother
I was not coerced into giving up my baby
I am not adopted; I look like my aunt, grandma etc.
I had no other children

All the above statements/questions serve to hide from one's real feelings, feelings that are so painful they cannot be endured until one gets help.

Victims of sexual assault often claim responsibility for the assault because that is less painful than remembering the feelings of hopelessness and helplessness and in the case of incest, less painful than believing that someone who was supposed to love them could also assault them. It is not surprising that mothers of adoption loss often claim responsibility for their situation for the same reasons.

One of the things that I have seen over the years is the difference of response upon being contacted by one's other to initiate a reunion. Mothers rarely say no, adoptees very often say no. I believe this is because our mothers remember, as painful as it is, what they survived. Adoptees have no *conscious* memory of what they survived so while being contacted can be terrifying, it is more terrifying for the adoptee as she has no idea what the pain looks like whereas moms do.

I am not comparing pain or one's ability to endure pain or the amount of pain. There *is* no way to compare these things. I am talking about the fear of one's pain and it is clear to me that in general, adoptees find it harder to do. This is why, in my opinion, adoptees can be more

> "Warding off early pain leads to amnesia about one's childhood... The thread to the child one once was is broken, leaving no trace of past experiences. Consequently, the wounded person is unable to experience her own feelings because her capacity to feel is no longer available to her." – *The Abandoned Child Within* – Kathryn Asper

difficult to deal with in reunion than mothers of adoption loss, and why adoptees find it harder to do the healing work. We must recognize that all of the pain of our losses is very, very severe, and I am not comparing as, and I repeat, there is no way to do so... I am only looking at one's ability to face it. To re-state it, mothers have a pre-traumatic self, a self that they can remember, a self that functioned in this world and the knowledge and memories of that "self" help her to face her pain. Adoptees do not have a pre-traumatic self and so facing her pain is harder for her. A mom can be reminded of that pre-traumatic self, that she knows what she survived, and sadly, an adoptee cannot be so reminded and this is why I spent six years, twice a week in therapy terrified to talk of adoption, even say the word for fear of instant annihilation. My fear, my terror of touching my trauma was typical of that of both moms and adoptees... the fear of instant annihilation. Yet, we can all break through bit by bit and heal.

How do we get help for PTSD?

First, we need to realize it exists.

Earlier I wrote about my experience after 9/11. I knew the trauma existed because I had dealt with my adoption trauma. It was easy for me to understand that I had experienced another trauma, was living in the aftermath of it, PTSD, and needed more help.

I had an earlier experience with trauma that I was unaware was a trauma until I began my adoption recovery work. Christmas of 1975, I was walking down 1st avenue in Manhattan when suddenly I heard this almost inaudible weird sound: thwup, thwup, thwup… followed by a clunk on the top of my head. My first instinct was that someone had thrown an ice cube at me; I grabbed my head, felt the wet and looked at a hand smeared with blood. I hailed a cab and raced to a nearby hospital ER.

By the time the physician came in and examined me, the bleeding had stopped and, he explained they wanted to be sure that there was no internal damage and ordered an x-ray. The results shocked me. The doctor told me that the x-ray showed a bullet lodged between my scalp and skull. Apparently the bullet entered about two inches above my right eye and traveled under the skin along the skull and settled approximately four inches above my ear. It was a miracle that the skull had not been penetrated. Ironically the bitter cold and wind that had me holding my head down, in essence was a life saver.

The police came to the ER as they are required to do for all gunshot wounds and after some further questioning and telling them of the location where I was injured, they revealed that a woman had been shot in the thigh by a roof top sniper on the same block earlier in the evening.

The physician did not believe I would need any further treatment, telling me that it was more dangerous to remove the bullet surgically than leaving it there to rest quietly... it would present no medical danger. (Strangely, I know two other male adoptees who were shot in the head by accident and survived.)

I had a very mild headache for a few days and occasionally when a storm was coming, my scalp itched where the bullet was sitting. I gave it no further thought. However, a few weeks later I was walking down 5th avenue and came to the large intersection at 57th street and suddenly I was terrified. I was into a full blown panic attack. I realized that I was afraid of being shot again. I looked up at the open space and wondered if a sniper was lurking, ready to shoot me again. I had no idea I had suffered a trauma or that I had PTSD. A few minutes later, away from that intersection, I had no conscious memory of the terror I had just experienced. It was gone. Unknown to me, PTSD was at work.

A year later I began my therapy, the twice-a-week, no-adoption-talk therapy, that lasted for six years. I never told my therapist about the shooting. Only after digging into my adoption trauma did it occur to me to talk about being shot and then the impact of this trauma become apparent. For years afterwards, I had avoided open spaces, always walking close to buildings, hurrying across intersections, unconscious of the trauma that controlled how I behaved on the street. Discussing this trauma brought up the other near death incidents, incidents where an inch or a few seconds meant the difference between life and death. I began to realize how the trauma of losing my mother at birth was compounded by a half-dozen newer traumas. I began, with the help of my shrink, to understand what I had truly survived. I began to be proud of my scars, they were proof of what I had survived and only by being aware of our trauma(s) can we heal. I stopped being afraid of open spaces, I stopped being afraid to fly, I stopped being afraid to live.

We may fight acknowledging the existence of our PTSD because of our fear. Once we acknowledge it, then, bit by bit we can try to talk about it in safe places with knowledgeable people. As we learn to talk about it, as painful and scary as it is, we come to understand that these feelings will not cause us to perish. We get comforted with validation, with words, perhaps hugs from those we want to hug us. The more we talk about it, the more we become desensitized to the thoughts of our trauma. The more we cry, the less we will need to cry; the more we talk about our anger, the less we will need to talk about our anger. The best therapists are those who have experienced the same type of trauma and worked it through in their own therapy. If they have not worked it through, they are unlikely to be able to help us. A mom should not need a mom therapist, nor should an adoptee need an adoptee for a therapist. A therapist who is a mom or an adoptee and who has done her work on her own trauma should be able to help any other adoptee or mom since I believe that we adoptees and moms share so much of our trauma on a cellular level.

Before we leave this chapter, it should be noted that traumatic events have a cumulative effect. The more traumas we experience that go untreated, the more severe our PTSD will be. Many of us do not recognize how many traumas we have experiences.

Moms have not only the trauma of the loss of their babies but may have the trauma of maternity home abuses, trauma of involuntary sterilization, sexual abuse and trauma of many unrecognized earlier and subsequent events.

Adoptees have the trauma of loss of their mothers, the trauma of "discovery" of adoptive status and the trauma of age of understanding. Add to that the all too common emotional and physical abuse and possible sexual abuse and there could be many layers of trauma that need to be addressed.

One abuse that is all too common is sexual abuse. The percentage of moms and adoptees (both male and female) who are sexually abused is staggering. Sexual abuse is often so well hidden that it never shows up but can affect the abusee in a myriad of ways. If you suspect you have been sexually abused, I suggest you read, "The Courage to Heal" by Bass. It may help you figure it out. As a victim of sexual abuse, this book helped me greatly and it led me to a secondary specialization of helping those who have been sexually abused. Working on sexual abuse issues can be just as terrifying as working on our adoption issues but it is vital that it be addressed.

Trauma victims often claim responsibility for the abuse. Moms will say they freely made a decision to not keep their child when, in fact, they did not have a choice. Victims of sexual abuse will commonly say they encouraged it or were to blame in some way, when by definition, victims of sexual abuse had no choice. Why take the blame? Why would someone insist it was her my fault? One common reason is because it's less painful then remembering the hopelessness and helplessness of the trauma. Adoptees will often (illogically and vehemently) take responsibility for their mother's pregnancy or for not being kept. Remember that children always blame themselves for what happens to them and once those thoughts occur to a seven or eight year old, they are fixed in cement until and if and when the adult does her healing work.

Clearly for moms and adoptees the accumulation of their traumas can be very hard to deal with... hard but very, very, do-able. One needs to make the commitment to do the work and follow through.

Just as a good tennis player needs to practice every day and an alcoholic may need to go to a 12-step meeting every day, we adoptees and moms need to do daily work to heal. Going to a support group once a month is not likely to be enough. Inner child work *must* be done daily. There are people I know who travel great distances to get to support group meetings. One mom and one adoptee I know came separately to my meetings, driving more than three hours each way.

Before I started Adoption Healing, I once took a plane from Dallas to NY, so I would not miss my monthly afternoon meeting at the local support group, and flew back to Dallas that same evening... I knew I needed it. So please don't sabotage your work by not doing it regularly. No matter what, find a way. Read, chat, go to meetings, journal, channel, and take care of your IC.

Channeling anger involves saying out loud in your head, "I am going to take my anger and use it to exercise, mow the lawn, etc." Saying this out loud in your head tells your unconscious mind to take untamed anger and use it to do the specified physical activity. One cannot channel sadness or pain, etc. Only anger.

Healing involves a lot of time and patience. I look at it as climbing a mountain of recovery. Each person's path up the mountain is different, the climb steep, but climbable, no matter what. There are many crevices and gullies on the way up, perhaps some abysses too, but each crevice, gully or abyss is still part of your path up the mountain and going down into it and up the other side is part of your path to freedom. Freedom from constant fear, pain, sadness and anger. When one stops being afraid of her emotions, one *is* truly free. Peace and contentment and happiness are the reward. Quiet Desperation can become Tranquility

Recently, someone told me they resented having to do this work and asked me how to get past the resentment. I asked her to imagine a mountain with a pile of gold at the top and would she resent having to climb up to the top to get the gold. "Heck no!", was the reply. "What would you feel about having to climb up to get it?", I asked. "I'd happily anticipate getting to the top, of course." I told her that long ago I was going to therapy three times a week at seven in the morning. That time slot was all that was available yet as much as I hate getting up that early, I truly looked forward to each session. I told her that my therapy was a trip up the mountain. Each session brought me closer to the "gold." She looked at me quizzically. I suggested that she look at her recovery as a trip up the mountain with a reward of gold at the top. The gold in this case is peace, contentment and freedom from the fear of all emotions. Happiness awaits at the so exchange the resentment for happy anticipation. You'll reap the rewards if you do.

To Summarize

+ The loss of a mother or child is a traumatic event
+ The sufferer will have Post Traumatic Stress Disorder or PTSD
+ PTSD is treatable.

Exercise

- Can you journal what you experienced on 9/11?
- Can you journal your feelings about your adoption loss?

Experience of the Moment

- You might be experiencing some tightness in your chest or some anxiety or pain. You might be feeling something undefinable. Can you write about it?

Chapter 1

I Feel Like a Hotdog

"Not to have knowledge of what happened before you were born is to be condemned to live forever as a child." - Cicero (c. 106-43 BC)

As far as I know, English is the only language in the world in which one can confuse feelings and thoughts. "I feel like a hot dog" is a thought, not an emotion. In every day communication this is not a problem but for our healing work the distinction between what we feel and what we think is of the utmost importance.

Why? Because we cannot simply change what we feel even though it is our desire to do so. However, as human beings, we can change what we think and when we do so, our feelings will change. For example, look at the back of a painting and take note of what you feel (your emotion) about the blank canvas/frame. Now look at the front of the painting and take note of what feelings are evoked by the work of art.

Myths:
- When there is an adoption, no one suffers.
- Feelings can be wrong.

Facts:
- Everyone involved in an adoption has many losses.
- Feelings by definition can never be wrong.

The thoughts that are evoked by what we see, create the feelings that we have about what we see. If we are not aware of our feelings, how can we truly know what we like or dislike? How can we know with whom we wish to be or what we wish to do if we are not in touch with our emotions?

Years ago, before my therapy, I was in a motor-scooter accident. I suffered a broken ankle and a lot of contusions. I blacked out for a few minutes and woke up to the EMT attendant lifting me into the ambulance. I asked why they were putting me in an ambulance. He said you've been hurt. I said, no, I'm not hurt. I'm fine. I was unaware of the pain. My body had gone into psychogenic shock, and had shut down my awareness of the physical pain to protect me. I was clueless but my going into shock was what allowed me to function. This is a similar mechanism to the psychological shock that protects us against the pain of separation of mother and child. We can be totally unaware on a conscious level that the pain exists. With physical pain, the shock wears off. After the scooter accident, the EMT said that I had been hurt and I believed her. With emotional pain, it may never wear off until we have someone help us understand what truly happened to us at the beginning. We may need an adoption EMT to help us do just that.

We adoptees and moms are very used to being unaware of what we feel. Our emotional shock is a defensive strategy created by our unconscious mind that helped us survive the trauma of the separation of mother and child and its aftermath.

When, in my regular meetings or chat I ask people to make a feelings statement, I often hear something like, "I feel like searching" or "I feel like I can't heal." "I feel like a hotdog" is as much a feelings statement as the other two in this sentence. They are all thoughts. "I feel like searching" means, I want to search which is a thought. "I feel like I can't heal" is a thought that means I don't think I can heal, and "I feel like a hotdog" means, I am hungry for a hotdog.

To make good decisions about anything, we need to become aware of the difference between what we think and what we feel.

The basic feelings words are, "Fear, Glad, Guilt, Jealousy, Mad, Sad, and Shame." Some of these feelings may be foreign to you because you were told they were wrong. Feelings are never wrong. Even though you may be afraid of them, please know that experiencing them is normal, healthy and not deadly.

If you don't know what you are feeling, try asking, "What am I feeling?" out loud in your head and listen to what your inner self responds.

To Summarize

- Hidden feelings are common for trauma survivors.
- To heal, we must be in touch with what we feel.
- To get in touch with what we feel, we need to be patient with ourselves.
- Our feelings will not destroy us if we let ourselves experience them.

Exercise

- Close your eyes and try to visualize your inner child.
- Out loud in your head, tell her that her feelings are always ok to tell you and that she will never, ever be punished by telling you what she feels. Tell her no one but you can see her or hear her and that she is safe.

Experience of the Moment

•   You might be feeling frightened and if so, try to journal why you are frightened and the thoughts that you are having. (If you think you are having no thoughts, know that that too, is a thought!)

Chapter 2

Affirmations the Easy Way

"One of the saddest things of all is that so many adoptees and moms are afraid to take the risk of healing which is necessary to pursue one's dreams" - Anon

Please do not visualize your Inner Child while doing the affirmations. It is not necessary and will distract you.

Say them out loud in your head without paying attention to the meaning of the words or why you are saying them.

As long as you believe intellectually that what you are saying is truthful, the affirmations will take hold.

Myths:

*   Inner Child work is psychobabble or mumbo jumbo.
*   Talking to myself by saying these affirmations is silly.

Facts:

*   Everyone in the world does Inner Child work without even knowing it.
*   We learn new words by repeating them. Affirmations are no different. We learn by repetition.

The affirmation for adoptees:

> "You are lovable. I know it doesn't feel that
> way. What happened to you was not your
> fault. We are okay!"

The affirmation for mothers:

> "You are not responsible for losing your baby.
> know it feels like you are. What happened to
> you was not your fault. We are okay!"

Say the affirmation out loud in your head every hour 4 times in a row, or every other hour 8 times in a row. It needs to be said about 60 times a day for one month to be effective. The total time to say it each day will be between 3 and 4 minutes.

> "Nothing is happening now. I know it feels like
> it, but I just checked and we are okay. Relax, we
> are safe!"

The Panic Attack affirmation only needs to be said in panic situations:

Look around you to be sure that you are not in physical danger, then say out loud in your head:

Repeat looking around and say it again if necessary!

Remember that we must believe (intellectually) what we say to our IC. We cannot lie to her. We need to tell her the truth that she cannot see, teach her what she does not know and give her her voice to dialog with our adult self so she can learn that she is ok.

To Summarize

- What we think generates our emotions.
- We can change the way we feel by helping our inner child understand the truth instead of what she mistakenly thinks is true.

Exercise

- Close your eyes and try to imagine that younger person you were when you suffered your adoption loss.
- Can you visualize giving her a hug?

Experience of the Moment

- You might be feeling sad or anxious right now. Can you journal your thoughts and the feelings attached to them?

Chapter 3

KaBoom

"People cannot endure inexplicable worthlessness"
- John D. MacDonald

It is very common for adoptees and mothers of adoption loss to have difficulty dealing with their anger. If one has not had help with anger it can seem nuclear and be terrifying to express.

Having no choice about losing a child to adoption or losing a mother to adoption is an angrifying event.

Anger is a cumulative emotion. Let's imagine that anger is represented by dominos. Each event that causes anger puts up a stack of dominos. Perhaps our

> Street lamp reaction: The slightest incident, remark, event or even a smudge on the side of a street lamp can be perceived by an adoptee or mother as a "rejection" or "abandonment" and can create simultaneous feelings of rage, terror, hatred, pain and sadness that to the sufferer have no cause. Our inner child plunges instantly into the depths of hell and is ready to explode; unaware of what is truly happening.

adoption loss puts twenty dominos on the stack. Other things in life cause anger but since many of us are not "trained" in healthy ways of dealing with anger, more dominos go on the stack. The stack gets higher and more unstable. Someone looks at us cockeyed or we "think" they do. We get street lamped. One more domino goes on the stack and KaBoom! The stack of dominos (our anger) is unstable and we explode. If we don't Discharge our anger the D goes in front of our anger and makes it Dangerous.

Many adoptees and moms talk about walking down a street or sitting in a restaurant and getting the urge to just throw a glass or break something or hit someone. This is Free Floating Anger. This is likely anger from the initial trauma and a sure sign that the dominos are too high.

I believe that only hearts free of rage can see objectively. I say this because I meet many adoptees who cannot get rid of the rage at their mothers for not keeping them. Their reunions are often tumultuous and the adoptees blame the moms for their difficulties. However, it is my belief that in any relationship, adoption related or not, if I have deep anger or rage at my "other", I will always be looking at my "other" through "anger colored glasses" and therefore not be able to be objective about our relationship. I will not be able to see my "other" clearly and may sabotage the relationship unwittingly. Our inner children will be in charge of our decisions about our relationship. As adoptees, we need to learn how to remove our core anger at our mothers to be able to have a chance at a good relationship. We need to help our IC lower the stack of dominos.

We need to learn how to express our anger in healthy ways. We need to know it's ok to say we are angry when things anger us. Emotions are never wrong. Even if caused by illogical thinking, if we feel it, it is valid. We need to express it in a polite way or the domino stack will grow.

Aside from expressing it verbally, we need to journal it, channel it and list it to get it out of our system. The more we express it, the more diminished it will become. We need to express it until we do not need to any more. As we express it, the dominos will be taken off the stack, most will disappear... some will remain but will be lying alongside each other, flat on the ground, there but not in any way harmful, simply inactive or tamed, but usable for channeling into physical activity.

Journaling is done by writing your thoughts and feelings about the incidents that anger you. The more you write, the more your anger will be released in a very healthy, non-destructive way.

Channeling anger is like having a bilge pump in a boat. If the pump is off, the boat will sink as water seeps in and accumulates. One can lessen or release anger by channeling it. To channel it, you need only say a few quick words out loud in your head. You do **not** have to feel it, or even know why it is there. You just need to know the anger exists. You need to say out loud in your head, for example, "I'm going to take my anger and use it to *exercise*" or "I'm going to take my anger and use it to *paint*", etc. Common activities that lend themselves to channeling are: doing your daily work, cleaning, doing the dishes, exercising, mowing the lawn, jogging, painting, playing music, walking, writing poetry, prose or music. Any physical activity will be useful to channel your anger. Although it may be tempting, you cannot channel your anger into reading a book, watching TV or listening to music. Sedentary activities just won't cut it. You may need to say (again, all of this is out loud in your head) I'm going to take my anger and use it to get up out of this chair (a jump start) and clean the house.

The more you channel, the better you will feel, the less anger will be a problem and the more energy you will have to live your life. When you are channeling your anger, you are really talking to your unconscious mind and asking it to do this chore for you and it will obey. You literally free up the energy that you were using to keep the anger under control and you also save the good energy that you would have used to do the chore otherwise. When you channel your anger on a regular basis which is many times a day, you will eventually not even have to say the words out loud in your head anymore. You will start to channel as a way of life, automatically and you will feel so much better.

Another way of dissipating anger is to make anger lists. Get a note book and write down every single thing you are angry about, no matter how picayune. Put a number from 1 to 10 by each item in the list to indicate how angry you are about that particular item. This will help validate your feelings. The more you list, the fewer dominoes will remain on the stack, the less anger will be within you.

Some common sticking points:

One of the things we need to do as adoptees is get in touch with our IC's anger at not being kept. Children cannot see the world in gray, only black and white so this may be difficult. What often happens is the adoptee says to me, "My IC is not angry" and changes the subject.

"How do you know this?", I ask.
"I can tell", says the adoptee.

The only way to know what our inner children think or feel is to ask them and have them tell us directly. If we try to guess or presume, we will short-circuit our work. We adoptees need to talk to our ICs and get them to express the Primal Wound anger that I believe must be present in their minds. If they don't express it, it will not go away and can easily sabotage our relationships, especially with our mothers at reunion. Sometimes the adoptee is terrified, without being aware of it, of this primal anger so this work may take a while and a lot of patience but it must be done. Once our IC acknowledges the anger, we can explain that our mothers had no choice, that it was not about us, and that it's ok to have anger but to move the anger to the fact that it happened (which is very difficult for a child to do) or to the circumstances that prevented our moms from keeping us, which is also difficult for a child to do. To repeat, this takes time and patience to accomplish. Our ICs can be very stubborn about this.

For a mom, the biggest sticking point I see is getting past anger at her child for being distant or non-communicative. Since, sadly, most adoptees do not prepare before they search, reunion usually (unconsciously), brings up all the emotions from the past, the rage, anger and sadness of losing mommy. The adoptee, who can be very open at the beginning of reunion, can suddenly put on the brakes without being aware of what is truly going on inside her. To a mom it's being, "rejected" but to the adoptee it's just being safe. Ironically, the more open a mom is at reunion, the more likely it is for the adoptee to run. The chapters on "Fear of Mommy Love" and "Conflict of Two Moms" will, hopefully, help to explain these reactions of adoptees, painful and anger provoking as they are, to the mom.

One of the things we all must do is to read as much as possible about the psychology of our "other" and stop deciding we know what is going on inside them. We are only learning ourselves about what makes us tick and if our "other" is not doing any self-work, we need to have a lot of patience. If we can remember that what we think creates what we feel and can see that the actions of our "other" is not about us but about their own wounds, fears and pains, then our own feelings of pain, anger and sadness will lessen a great deal.

What we need to do is stop taking things personally, give our "other" lots of space and do our own work. The more we work on our own healing, the better able we will be to communicate to others in ways that may work.

And, no matter what, we will be healing.

To Summarize

- Anger is a normal human emotion.
- We need to find healthy ways to express our anger and tame it so it is not a destructive force in our lives

Exercise

- Close your eyes and hand your inner child some magic markers and paper to draw on. Ask her to draw a picture of her anger. Remind her that only you will be able to see it and she will not get in trouble for what she draws. She'll usually show you very quickly a representation of her anger on paper. (At other times, you might ask her to draw her sadness as well. If you are in therapy or a group, take

40

Joe Soll

the drawing to your therapist or group meeting.)

- Close your eyes and try to imagine saying out loud in your head, to someone important in your life, "I am angry because you do not understand me" then imagine that person saying, "I'm glad you told me you are angry. I will try to understand!"

Experience of the Moment

- Can you journal how you feel after you tried expressing your anger out loud in your head? Be as explicit as you can be. Try to journal your response to your IC's drawing in the exercise above.

Chapter 4

Baloney!

"The prisoner disintegrated because he could never find out what he was guilty of" - The Trial by Kafka

Why do adoptees and moms say "Baloney!" so often when I try to explain the actions/behavior/thoughts/feelings of their other?

I think that the reasons are ***unconscious*** and powerful.

Specifically:

Why do moms and adoptees often find it hard to understand that the behavior of their other could be the result of the trauma of losing each other?

I think that a mom would prefer to believe her child is uncaring rather than to believe her child was damaged by losing her. Her guilt may sky-rocket if she accepts this. Also if she can "de-value" her child by thinking her child is just not a nice person, then she didn't "lose" so much by being separated from her child.

I think that an adoptee would prefer to believe her mom is uncaring rather than to believe her mom was damaged by losing her. It fits the adoptees belief that she is unlovable and unworthy. Also if she

42

can "de-value" her mom by thinking her mom is just not a nice person and didn't love her in the first place, then she didn't "lose" so much by being separated from her mom.

To accept the truth, we have to fully grieve the loss of our "other" and on the surface that is much more painful.

On the surface these two "belief systems" diminish pain. But in reality they both cause more pain.

Why are adoptees and moms so prone to blaming their other for their behavior?

Unless we have read a lot about the trauma inflicted on ourselves and our other by adoption loss, it is hard to understand the psychological forces that affect one's behavior. And, most adoptees and moms are used to being blamed for their behavior so there is a built in mechanism for blaming others.

We are all victims of adoption loss and victims should not be blamed. Victims should be given help.

To accept the truth about someone's behavior, we have to fully grieve the loss of that person and on the surface that is much more painful.
On the surface blaming diminishes pain. But in reality, refusing to believe the truth causes more pain.

Why do adoptees find it so hard to believe their mom had no choice?

Sometime last century I had begun dating a young woman. I care for her very much. One day she came to me and said she could not see me anymore because she just found out that she was pregnant from her relationship with her last boyfriend. I asked why that meant she could not see me anymore. She said, "Because you know I am pregnant. I had to tell you but now that you know, I can't face you again." And that was that. I think of her often, wondering what she did. Adoption? Abortion? Keeping was out of the question but I didn't know about the way moms were treated until I came out of my adoption closet. When I started to meet mothers of adoption loss, I thought back to Barbara... "*so that's the way it was for her back then and why she could not see me again!*"

For an adoptee who did not know someone who went through the humiliation, shame, brainwashing, etc., that pregnant women were subjected to, it can be very difficult to accept someone having no choice.

> "I was 17 and unmarried, unsupported and terrified.
> You offered me only your vilification and scorn and
> plotted to take my baby from me." - Lina Eve

When my therapist suggested to me that there were reasons why a mother might not be able to keep her baby, I literally screamed, **"Bullshit! There is No Excuse for her not keeping me. None!"** It was not until I met moms and listened to the abuses they suffered that I finally understood. I then remembered Barbara and then also remembered high school and, "The Girls Who Went Away."[3] One day they were just gone. No explanation ever.

We adoptees must learn by reading and talking to moms. We have no right to judge them or what it was like for them. We did not walk in their shoes. We need to accept that what they tell us is the truth. The societal brainwashing of mothers is expertly done and continues today.

To accept the truth about the lack of choice of our mothers, we have to fully grieve the loss of that person and on the surface that is much more painful. We have to accept that we *were* loved and cared for and that is also more painful than continuing to believe what we were "programmed" to believe, that we were just throwaways, unwanted, uncared for and unloved.
On the surface not blaming diminishes pain. But in reality refusing to believe our moms causes more pain.

---

[3] I highly recommend you read, "The Girls Who Went Away" by Ann Fessler.

Why do adoptees and moms find it hard to believe that their "other cares about them and loves them?

To accept the truth, we have to fully grieve the loss of our "other" and on the surface that is much more painful. To do this grieving, we have to recognize the enormity of the loss of the mother/child relationship; the sacredness of that most powerful of all the forces in nature, that we have lost because of adoption; the trauma caused by that separation.

On the surface, believing our other doesn't care or love us allows us to devalue them as human beings, meaning we lost less and that means less pain and it means we do not have to grieve. But in reality this "devaluation" causes more pain because it reinforces our worthlessness as mothers or adoptees.

We need to feel and grieve the loss of our "others" to feel loved and cared about. Yes, we have to take the risk of losing the love and caring but, I've never met a mom or an adoptee who wanted to endure the loss of their other again. And, if we do not take that risk, we are cheating ourselves out of one of life's wonderful treasures.

Why do some friends, strangers, adoptive parents and even some other adoptees and mothers of adoption loss say "Baloney!" when we express our pain?

When it's another adoptee or mother of adoption loss, my belief is it's denial or repression of the pain. It's just too painful to contemplate. I do not believe that anyone can lose a mother or a child and not suffer from the trauma of that loss. But I suspect that many if not most cannot touch it enough to do the kind of work we are talking about in this book. It's just too terrifying. We need to recognize that we, who dare to face our demons, are the strong ones, super strong in fact but, more about that later.

When we are talking about strangers, friends or adoptive parents, I think something else is going on unconsciously. I live near one of the largest shopping malls in the country. A few years ago I was entering the mall and a bus-load of children from a local rehab hospital was unloading a few dozen kids suffering from what appeared to be cerebral palsy. They were sitting in wheel chairs with their heads off to the side, wrists twisted, faces in grimaces and I wanted to get away from them as fast as I could. I walked very fast until I was far away and sat down ashamed of myself.

A light bulb went off in my head. Why did I want to run away from those kids? Simple. My mind could not tolerate the thought of me being like them. Being confined to a wheel chair, twisted up, in pain, confusion, perhaps never being able to live a normal life... That was unthinkable. And I had an AHA moment. I wonder if those who do not want to hear of the pain of the loss of a mom or child cannot contemplate or tolerate in any way the thought of what it would be like to be one of "us." Why else would people deny our pain and suffering? I don't know if I am right but I think it's a strong possibility.

To Summarize

• To understand and accept the behavior of others, to not take it personally, to not judge or blame, we have to fully grieve the loss of our "other", a painful process. To do this grieving, we have to recognize the enormity of the loss of the mother/child relationship; the sacredness of that most powerful of all the forces in nature that we have lost because of adoption; the trauma caused by that separation.

• For others to accept that we were hurt by our adoption experience, to have empathy for us, they have to be willing to project what it would be like to experience what we have and that maybe be too painful to even contemplate.

Exercise

- Close your eyes and try to imagine what it would be like if you were disabled in some way and had to live your life without one of your senses. What if you lost the ability to see or hear or walk? What goes on in your mind when you try to imagine this? Perhaps it will help you understand why you say "Baloney"

Experience of the Moment

- Ask your IC what she thinks about what you have just read. Try to journal what your IC just responded.

Chapter 5

Walls

*"I never gave them hell. I told them the truth and they thought it was hell!" -
Harry S. Truman*

Why do so many adoptees and mothers of adoption loss seem distant? Or stop communication? Or not communicate at all? Why do they avoid talking about feelings and only talk about the "weather", etc.? Why do *we* always take it personally?

The answer is usually painfully, tragically simple... to avoid the pain of the truth. The horrors of the loss suffered by the separation caused by adoption. Any contact with our "other" brings forth the feelings of the loss of that person. Consciously or unconsciously the pain is there, so the terror is alongside it. If I am being real, I have to "touch" the pain of losing that person and the pain of the fear of losing that person again. These thoughts are terrifying. They are like living in hell.

We may do all sorts of things to avoid these feelings and thoughts. We may drink, cut ourselves, and lash out at others. We may just "turn off" and be emotionally numb. We need to have great respect for our fears, but to truly live, we must find a way to face our fears, experience our pain, and grieve our losses. We must do this in a safe way, and bit by bit we will see that our pain will not destroy us. We may need to put our toe in the water and test it, then maybe our foot, then our ankle, and so on until we know we will be able to stand the water of our emotional pain. Once we feel safe enough to experience our pain and do our grieving, we will stop having to act out (or act in) our emotions. Experiencing them and expressing them removes the need for the destructive ways of showing them.

We must not blame our other or ourselves for putting up the walls. We must have great empathy for the terrors, and understand that no one can just decide to stop being terrified. We must have patience until they or we are willing to dare to open the door and peek in.

Door? What door?

Imagine that you walk into your bedroom and you see a door on the far side of the room, a door that you've never seen before. There are flashes of light from under the door and you hear strange noises, rattling of chains, sounds of wings flapping, and blood curdling screams. What would you do? Could you ever sleep in this room with that door in it? Would you have to move to another house? And, what if a door showed up in the new house? How long could you wait before you turned the knob, prayed, held your breath and pushed open the door, just a fraction of an inch and then a bit more? And lo and behold you see a table and on that table is an old, black and white TV set playing a classic horror movie. Phew. Something from the past that we are afraid to look at. It only has power if we give it that power by not looking. Once we are brave enough to look, the past loses its power over us.

I used to think that to go to war and not be afraid was brave. Then a friend clued me in. If I go to war and am not afraid, I am not brave. I am stupid. If I am afraid to go into battle and do it anyway, *then* I am brave. For us to be afraid to do this healing work and do it anyway, that is truly a sign of bravery.

Find a safe way to take a peek, knowing that when you do so, you will be setting in motion the path to freedom. Know you are brave to do so. Be proud of it.

"Our terrifying feelings, sitting on the other side of the closed door in the dark, without love or light, have taken on a life of their own, and in a horrible twist of denial, a part of them believes that you are their enemy. They resist coming forward. They resist trusting you, and sometimes resist the very movement that is their only salvation. They have been judged by mind and spirit and the world. They have been tortured and maimed and killed any time they moved toward expression. They have been made to believe that any movement will bring down the wrath of God once again. And their fears are real. Give them as much reassurance as you can when you call to them, as much gentleness as you can." - Why Can't I Cry? From Our Pathway Home

Food for thought. We are all survivors of the highest order. Think of the terror you have now. Now, I'd like you to remember that you had these same terrors, the same pain that you are afraid of now, way back at the beginning when you endured the losses and you survived without any help from anyone. Now, I'd like you to be aware that if you could survive back then without any help from anyone, survive as the young mother you were or the young child you were, you can surely survive now with support. Many people do not survive the losses we have experienced. They wind up on the streets, or in a bottle or worse and can't get out. (Addiction is, sadly, common among PTSD victims... a way to hide from the pain.) But you are here, today, working on your healing, willing to face your pain. You survived your trauma way back then without help. You can do it now with help. I know it's scary but you have proof you can do this. . .

You've already done it!

To Summarize

•   We are all survivors. We may have difficulty looking at ourselves that way, but we are here, proof that we have survived.

- We can heal. All we need is a commitment to do so.

Exercise

- Think of someone you know who is afraid to do this work. What is the difference? What in *you* allows you to be on this healing path?

Experience of the Moment

- Make a list of your strengths in your journal. Think very hard and do not be modest.

Chapter 6

When Your Inner Child Doesn't Talk

"Emotional sickness is avoiding reality at any cost. Emotional health is facing reality at any cost." - M. Scott Peck

Imagine you are walking through an airport terminal or in a shopping mall, and you come across a child who is crying for mommy... scared, lonely, angry, and afraid to trust. Afraid to respond!

I'd like you to think of your inner child that way. She needs you to understand he feelings of pain, anger and sadness. You need total empathy for your inner child; the child you once were. Remember that she never did anything wrong. She

> "Three things are striking about inner child work: the speed with which people change when they do this work; the depth of that change; and the power and creativity that result when wounds from the past are healed." – *Homecoming* – John Bradshaw

was helpless and had no choice so she deserves total empathy. Treat your IC as you would the lost, terrified child in the airport or mall.

Remember, too, that your IC has no reason to trust anyone. Her sense of trust was severely hampered by her loss. It will take time for her to trust you. So, the more you visit her, talk to her, calm her, let her have the opportunity to talk without fear of reprisals, the sooner she will be able to trust you.

Do some soul searching and try to find out if you are angry with your IC or afraid of her. Remember that your IC did nothing wrong. She was a victim and needs to be cherished. If you are afraid of her, ask yourself why. How could she possibly hurt you? What I often hear is that people are afraid of their IC's pain. Our IC's pain is our pain and if we don't help our Inner Children, that hidden, unaddressed pain will continue to affect us forever. Just as a toothache treated with Orajel only stops the pain and allows the decay to continue, our hidden untreated feelings allow emotional decay to occur within us. Having total empathy for our IC has to be a priority for us to heal. When I say, "Don't touch that tooth", that IS the tooth that needs attention.

If you are angry with or afraid of your IC, she will know it and avoid you, just as any other person would do.

I suggest that you talk to your IC a minimum of two times a day. Doing it while you brush your teeth might make it easier to get in the habit of doing so.

Tell your IC that no one can see her but you, no one can hear her but you and no one can touch her but you. Tell her she is safe, no one can ever punish her. Tell her that all her feelings are ok to say to you... that feelings are never wrong

Your IC may not want to talk to you for some time but please know she is always listening. Tell her that she can trust you and that if she has any doubts to look in your heart. (Inner Children have the ability to do just that.)

Be patient. Ask her if she would rather write instead of talk for now and if she says, or nods yes, give her magic markers and paper. Tell her as often as you can that you love her and that you are on call 24/7.

To Summarize

•   Think of your IC as a terrified, lonely younger you, desperately wanting love and comfort.
•   Treat her the way you would any young person in need.

Exercise

•   Write down your feelings about your IC. If you have anger towards her or are afraid of her, what can you do to change your feelings about her?
•   Try to visualize her at the moment of her adoption loss. What was she feeling way back then? Journal your thoughts and feelings.

Experience of the Moment

•   You might have confusing feelings about your IC right now. Try to journal as much as you can about this.

Chapter 7

Preparation for Searching: Why?

"Guilt is the most useless of human emotions... It is worrying today about something that happened yesterday and cannot be changed." - Anon

When people come to me for search help, the first thing I say is that for me to guide them, they must prepare.

"Prepare for what?", they ask.

"For whatever happens... in that way it will be a win-win."

Then I hear:

"How can I know what to prepare for?"
"I'm prepared, I've been waiting for 20 years."
"When I find my mom or my child, all will be well."

The fact is that no one can just be prepared for search and reunion.

It usually takes four to six months of concentrated effort. Part of the preparation is to work on our own pain, anger and sadness first. Reunions won't end our suffering, only hard work will.

I am obligated both ethically and legally to not help anyone who will not prepare. The reason is simple: Non-preparation can be both hurtful and dangerous. The searcher can be hurt emotionally and so can the person found if we do not handle ourselves well. The searcher and/or the person found can be so emotionally moved as to do something physically self-injurious.

I say this not to scare but to forewarn. Those who prepare will always be all right.

The fact is that to have survived the trauma of the loss of a mother or child, we all had to bury a myriad of very painful thoughts and feelings.

Searching will open us up to those very thoughts and feelings that we had to hide from.

If we talk about what we feel before we search, talk through our pain, anger and sadness, then we will be ready for anything that occurs.

We need to read about our other. We adoptees need to understand the experience of our mothers and mothers need to understand the experience of adoptees. We need to talk with other adoptees and moms. Share with them and learn from them.

We need to do our inner child work. We all have a hurt younger self that is very vulnerable and needy. Search is not the answer but our inner child usually thinks it is. Our healing has to come from our adult self nurturing our inner child.

We need to understand our obligation to those whom we find. We need to understand how they might react and why.

We need to grieve the loss of our "other" in advance. Admittedly it is difficult to grieve in advance, but we can do it by helping our inner child to express her emotions.

We need to do this work in a safe way. We need to go to support group meetings, participate in chat, read the books, talk, feel, journal and do inner child work at a speed that is comfortable.

Private therapy cannot prepare one. Private therapy can be a good side dish but cannot take the place of interacting with other moms and adoptees.

This work needs to be done with "enlightened witnesses" or "loving witnesses" who are there for us when we get into pain, anger and sadness. It takes time to build trust within your support group so be patient and allow this to happen.

We must not watch the clock. It takes as long as it takes. I look at this work as climbing a mountain of recovery and each person's path up the mountain is different. Each person's path has gullies, canyons, dips, and rises but those down turns are not failures, just part of one's particular path up the mountain.

In many ways, the journey is more important than the end result since the answers do not heal us, only the journey can and will. If we do it!

I look at preparation as being in flight school, learning how to fly. No one is allowed to fly until they have completed ground school and performed the check lists along with their instructor. The prep work is ground school. Your enlightened witnesses are you co-pilots. No prudent pilot tries to take off without doing the check list. Those who do not perform their check list before searching are likely to crash and burn. In almost 30 years of helping others, I have never once heard anyone who prepared say they wished they had not searched. Not Once!

To Summarize

---

* Preparation for search is a must.
* If we prepare, we are guaranteed a win-win.

Exercise

• Close your eyes and imagine contacting your "other" for the first time.

Experience of the Moment

• Journal your feelings about meeting your "other."

Chapter 8

The "R" Word

"Guilt is the most merciless disease of man. It stains all the other areas of living. It darkens all skies" - *John D. MacDonald*

When facilitating my support groups or nightly chat or in a session with one of my clients, I often hear someone say that they are afraid of getting "rejected" again. This is referring to what might happen if one searches and gets turned down, or if a reunion goes awry.

> "The primary or core issues for adoptees are abandonment and loss. From these two issues, the issues of rejection, trust, intimacy, loyalty, guilt and shame, power and control, and identity emanate." Nancy Verrier, **Primal Wound**

As adoptees, what we need to understand is that we were not "rejected" when we lost our mothers. The adoption arrangements were made before we were born, when our mothers didn't even know us! Many moms were not allowed to see or hold their babies. But we adoptees take it personally and "know" that it had to be something unlovable about us. We need to understand that all babies are lovable, without exception and therefore, no matter what happened it was not rejection. For me to be rejected there has to be something about me that is not likeable, not lovable. Since all babies are lovable then I could not have been rejected. If a mother, for some reason does not love her baby, that is about the mom. It cannot be about her baby, so it cannot be rejection. The pain of adoption loss is just as profound for a mom as it is for an adoptee. We all survive our losses by pushing them away. When a mom is contacted, the hidden feelings of pain, anger and sadness start knocking at her consciousness. If she cannot face her hidden feelings because they are so terrifying then she may not be able agree to contact. When someone is truly terrified they usually do not have the ability to confront their fears. This works both ways and we need to respect the feelings of someone who is truly terrified that their feelings will destroy them.

If I choose to search and when I make contact, I am turned down by my mother (or in the case of a mom searching turned down by the child she lost to adoption) that is not rejection of me but an unwillingness of the person found to face her pain. It cannot be about the searcher because the searcher is unknown to the person found. Aside from the terror of facing her pain, a mom might fear severe consequences from her family members who may not know her secret.

Now comes the inner child work. What we think affects how we feel. The words I say about myself, the words I think about myself greatly affect my emotions. If I can stop thinking the "R" word, if I can remove the word "rejection" from my vocabulary, then I can do what I want with impunity because I know that: #1 I was not rejected at birth, and #2, I cannot get rejected if I should choose to search for my family. I can get told, "No", and that would be sad, but it would not be devastating because it would not be a "rejection" of me.

No matter what we do, being told, "No", will be horribly sad and hurt like hell. However, if I've done my inner child work, in the end, knowing that it's not a "rejection" of me, that it's not about me at all, it's about the other party's own experience and feelings is what makes the difference. Part of the preparation for search is to be aware of all the things that can happen, both good and bad. If we do this preparation along with the inner child work, no matter what happens, we will be ok. Yes, we may hurt like hell but we will be ok.

I often hear, "I feel rejected, or I feel abandoned." To be clear, abandoned and rejection are not feelings. They are thoughts based on our past experience, thoughts that create great anguish. If we can recognize this and do the thought changing work of this chapter, we will remove a lot of anguish from our lives. If I hear myself thinking, "I feel rejected" and stop a moment and ponder... "Am I being rejected? Am I being abandoned?", I will usually see that neither of those thoughts is true. Also, adults can't be abandoned. To truly be abandoned, one has to be left in a position from which she cannot survive. I suspect that none of us need to worry about that happening. Yes, someone can leave us and that would be sad, but it's not abandonment. Usually these thoughts are the thoughts of our IC so we immediately need to go to our IC and reassure her that what she fears is not happening and cannot happen. As trauma victims our inner core expects the past to repeat. As adults, we need to be aware that what happened at the beginning cannot possibly repeat as we are adults now and in charge of our lives.

For us to make the above changes, the first step is to intellectually know that all babies are lovable and then make sure our inner child accepts this as fact.

Next we have to do the intellectual work of knowing that we were not rejected at the beginning and then make sure that our inner child knows that she was not rejected at the beginning.

Next we have to intellectually understand that we cannot get rejected if we search and then make sure our inner child knows that. The inner child work I refer to consists of our "talking" out loud in our head to our seven year old self (for an adoptee) and telling her/him the intellectual truth that it was not rejection in the past and cannot be rejection now. To do this, we have to have previously done the work of helping our inner child know that she/he was lovable and still is.

If we do this, we will be at a place to never fear losing a relationship ever again. Sure, it is sad to lose relationships, but when one knows it cannot be a 2nd rejection, one is free of one of the biggest adoption issues we all face. I'm not saying this is easy. It takes a lot time and a lot of work, but the payoff is a wonderful reward.

Please do me a favor. Throw out the "R" word. It will change your life.

To Summarize

- Rejection is not a feeling.
- We can be told "No" but we cannot get rejected when we search.
- We can stop being afraid of being abandoned

Exercise

- Close your eyes and find your IC. Tell her everything you have learned in this chapter.
- What is IC's response? . Does she believe you? If not, ask her what she would need from you to believe you. Journal what she says.

Experience of the Moment

- What are you feeling right now? Does your adult self understand everything in this chapter? If there are things you are unclear about, please re-read the chapter and then make a list of things you don't understand. Bring the list to your group/therapist/chat, etc.

Chapter 9

Special, Chosen and Lucky

"All children behave as well as they are treated." - anon

How many times do we adoptees hear those three words?
They are presumably said with all good intentions, what goes on inside us when we hear them?

If I am special, do I have to follow the rules?
If I am chosen, did I come from a baby supermarket? Why did they pick me?
If I am lucky, what makes me so?
If I am special, why was I available to be chosen?
If I was chosen, did someone un-choose me first?
If I am lucky, why do I hurt so much inside?
If I am special, why does it not feel good when I hear it?
If I am chosen, who were the other contestants?
If am lucky, does that mean my first family was "bad" in some way?

Each time someone says one of those words, it is a reminder that we are adopted. The intent is to make us feel good, not hurt, not think about our natural mothers. Yet each time we hear these words, how can we not on some level think of where we came from? It's like telling us to not think of pink elephants. Each time we hear the words it causes us internal pain. We may not be conscious of it, but it has to be there.

63

The reason why we adoptees do so much day-dreaming (which to the uninformed mental health professionals looks like ADD) is because we are constantly (at least unconsciously) trying to figure it all out. Who and why the biggest unanswered questions and our minds struggle to understand what no one can or will tell us.

There are phobic and counter-phobic reactions to pain and fear.
The phobic adoptee tells no one they are adopted.
The counterphobe flaunts being adopted, tells others how special she or he is.

In reality, the loss of our mothers at birth was a trauma of the highest order that is worse than "the horrors of war." - Anna Freud

Each time we hear one of those three words, that trauma is stirred up. When we are separated from our mothers we experience their death. There is no difference in losing a mother to death or adoption. Mommy is here, mommy is gone. Poof! Death as far as the infant's experience goes.

If we are special, does that mean it is good to lose a mom?
If we are chosen, does that mean our parents took us from our mothers on purpose?

If we are lucky, does that mean we are lucky our mothers are dead for us?

I like to throw away words that hurt, like the "R" word... Rejection

Maybe we should throw these three words away as well.

Spread the word, throw out "S", "C" and "L" because they are not what they say they are.

To Summarize

•   The words we hear have a tremendous effect on us.

- Although well meaning, the use of Special, Chosen and Lucky does not give comfort.

Exercise

- Journal what you used to feel when you heard those words, Special, Chosen and Lucky. Talk to your IC about these words and write down what she says.

Experience of the Moment

- What are you feeling now? What impact do those words have on you today? Can you understand why you feel the way you feel? Would you like to change these feelings?

Chapter 10

Fear of Mommy Love

"The only way around is through" - Robert Frost

Years ago, a 60 year old adopted woman joined my weekly support group meeting. Her first words were, "I want to search for my mom... I know how to deal with 'rejection' but what if she accepts me? I don't know if I could handle that." And she started to sob.

What is this really about? Over the years I've heard so many adoptees express, directly or indirectly that they were afraid of being loved, especially by their natural moms. How could this be so? Why would anyone be afraid of being loved by anyone? And by their own mother?

I remember when my own therapist said she loved me. I wanted to crawl inside the couch in terror. Thank God she understood and helped me understand.

We adoptees lost the most sacred and intense love relationship in the world. The reasons why don't matter. What does matter is that we lost what we needed the most psychologically, physiologically and spiritually. On some level we always knew it was missing and always longed to have that love.

As a child it would have been easy to "re-connect" and feel it. However, if as an adult I allow myself to feel the love of my mother, I have four (usually unconscious) problems.

1. Recognizing this as an issue can be terrifying in and of itself.

2. If I let myself feel it, I will feel what I always wanted and what was always missing and the pain of that thought can be terrifying.

3. Terrifying as well, is the anger that surfaces when I see what I lost. I fear I will either explode in rage or die from the pain.

4. Trauma victims (the loss of the mother/child relationship is a trauma of the highest order) always believe the trauma will repeat itself so, if I let myself feel it, my mother will leave again and I will die.

This fear of mommy love can sabotage a reunion in the blink of an eye without anyone being aware of what is really going on under the surface. Moreover, if I am afraid to be loved by my own mother, I may well have difficulties letting anyone truly love me.

This is not a message of doom. We can overcome our fears.

My method of doing this kind of work is Inner Child work. (IC)

1. We must help our IC understand that she/he was and is lovable.

2. We must help our IC grieve the loss of the mommy/child relationship.

3. We must help our IC understand that she/he will not die from feeling mommy love, even though it "feels" like it.

4. We need to trust that our mothers will not leave again, that they do not want to experience this trauma again any more than we do.

5. We need to realize that even if our mothers leave again, we will not die. We are not babies anymore; we are adults and will survive. We survived that loss as a baby without any help from anyone so surely we can survive as mature adults.

> "The baby who cannot get her mother back, despite her cries (protesting her disappearance and beseeching her return) is helpless, overwhelmed, thrown into chaos, and eventually goes into shock. [It takes about 45 minutes for an infant separated from her mother to go into shock. [Primal Wound rage at the separation] After rage comes despair then shock. This helplessness turns to hopelessness and a belief that the world is not safe. One cannot trust. Defenses against any future reoccurrence of these traumas [possible abandonment] are being put into place, many of which are almost impossible to eradicate from the psychological/neurological system."
> - Nancy Verrier, **Coming Home to Self**

This work takes time, effort and commitment. However, if we can do the work, we will be more able to let the important people in our lives truly love us and we will come alive in ways that we never thought possible.

We will be able to live our lives in happy, healthy ways.

Spring is here, time for renewal. How about giving yourself this gift of feeling loved?

To Summarize

- Most adoptees have a deep seated, unconscious fear of being loved by anyone, especially their original mother.
- This fear stems from losing one's mother.

Exercise

- Try to intellectually grasp that what happened in the beginning cannot happen again, no matter what. If you doubt this intellectually, journal the reasons for your disbelief.

Experience of the Moment

- Are you afraid right now? Anxious? Can you get in touch with why? Look around you and do the anti-panic attack affirmation. Nothing is happening now, right? Recognize how powerful these fears are. Recognize that you doing this work because you want to change the way these feelings affect you. Recognize that change is possible.

Chapter 11

Conflict of Two Moms: Adoptee's Dilemma

"There are ex-husbands and ex-wives but there are no ex-moms, ex-dads or ex-children." - Anon

Our first moms need to accept that we can love our adoptive moms.

Our adoptive moms need to accept that we can love our first moms.

We adoptees need to accept that we can love both moms.

As adoptees we are usually socialized to believe we can only love one mother, yet we are told we are adopted and that our first mother couldn't or wouldn't keep us or is dead etc., and that is supposed to be the end of it. But it cannot be. Bonding is a physiological and psychological process that begins in the womb and one part of the process is that babies are born loving their mothers. Then how could we not think about them? Why can't we love both of them?

Since to children growing up, their mothers are all powerful goddesses, children believe they know everything. Therefore to an adopted child growing up, if they think about their first mom with love, their adoptive mom will know, get angry, and throw them out. The adoptee knows she lost her first family for some reason and doesn't want to be "re-abandoned" no matter what. So, the adoptee has to stop thinking or asking about her first mom. To complicate matters, if the adoptee thinks about her adoptive mom with love, her first mom will know and not return. All of the above is usually unconscious, and causes a powerful conflict that is impossible to resolve. It gets buried.

Skip forward to adulthood. If the adoptee can overcome the fear of "abandonment" enough to search, the process and hopefully reunion will trigger the conflict of two moms, and an inner battle of loyalty will often ensue. If I love this one, that one will "reject" me and vice versa.

> "An uninterrupted continuum of being within the matrix of the mother is necessary in order for the infant to experience a rightness or wholeness of self from which to begin his separation or individuation process. The continuity and quality of this primal relationship is crucial because it may set the tone for all future relationships."
> - Nancy Verrier, **Primal Wound**

To further complicate matters, it's common for our adoptive parents to be terrified that we will leave them for our first parents.

Plus:

Our adoptive moms are often jealous of the love we have for our first parents.

Our first moms often jealous of the love we have for our adoptive parents.

Our adoptive moms are often jealous of the fact that our first moms gave birth to us.

Our first moms are jealous of our adoptive moms because they got to raise us.

Our adoptive moms are often angry at our first moms because they gave birth to us.

Our first moms are often angry at our adoptive moms because they got to raise us.

And the adoptee is caught in the middle of this very powerful, emotional conflict. For the adoptee, the usually unconscious struggle seems like life and death. If I choose a relationship with my first mom over my adoptive mom, I will surely die. The fear is that terrifying and no logic in the world can get most adoptees past that without help. Also, most adoptees have rage at their first mom for leaving in the beginning and cannot trust, no matter what they are told, that their first mom won't leave again. It is often, again unconscious, fear of being loved by their first mom that tips the loyalty scales towards their adoptive mom. This is not about who one loves more, but who is safer to one's inner child who is terrified about being left again.

This conflict can be assuaged for the adoptee if she is willing to dig into the conflict with some inner child work.

For the two moms, understanding the adoptee conflict will lessen their confusion and pain.

For all involved, we need to understand that we adoptees can love two moms without lessening the love one has for the other.

To Summarize

- Most adoptees have an unconscious conflict with their feelings about their two mothers.
- This conflict can "feel" life threatening.

72

Exercise

- Visualize your IC. Tell her that feelings are never wrong and that it is ok to have whatever feelings she has about her two moms. Tell her that neither mom will know what she feels about the other. Tell her that even if it seems to be the case, neither mom is a mind-reader. Tell IC she is safe.

Experience of the Moment

- You might be experiencing some fear that one or both of your mothers is tuned in to your feelings and thoughts. Your thoughts are your own, private, and no one can peek inside. You and your IC are safe. Hug your IC and remind her of that.

Chapter 12

Her Absence Filled My World

"The past isn't dead...........It isn't even past" - William Faulkner

Recently, one of my clients made me aware of a painting by William Kentridge entitled "Her Absence Filled the World." I googled it, found it on line and it moved me greatly.

It is a black and white scene, desolate, with a figure standing on a hill, almost at the top. An animal, perhaps a cat, sits at her side, with faint shadows of other people off to the side. Through therapy I came to know that on some deep level the absence of my mother was always on my mind, too terrifying to be aware of except for fleeting moments which were then repressed. One member of my support group referred to it as her background sadness.

I now think it is more than that, much more. Just as the world of someone whose loved one is missing in action is constantly aware of their absence, their hearts and minds filled with worry, despair... obsessed with thoughts, conscious and unconscious, of the missing person, finding it difficult to think of anything else, so too, do we who have someone missing in adoption, have their absence filling our world.

There is a big difference, however. Those who have a loved one missing in action have their concerns acknowledged by society, their friends and relatives. On the other hand, those of us who have someone missing in adoption do not have our losses sanctioned by society. We are encouraged or instructed to "Get Over It" or make believe we do not have anyone missing. This lack of sanction or disenfranchisement of our grief makes it worse.

> "You shoved a pillow in front of my face and I thought,
> 'I must be giving birth to some kind of hideous monster.'
> I didn't know this was a hospital policy to try to
> stop me from bonding with my baby." - Lina Eve

Imagine being in an accident and having a compound fracture of your leg, bone sticking out through the skin. You are taken to the hospital in excruciating pain, put on a bed and forgotten about. No pain killers, no treatment. What would you feel? Rage at not being tended to? (Which literally make your physical pain worse.) Feelings of despair, helplessness, sadness? And somewhere in your mind would be the most spoken phrase when someone is dying, "I want my mommy!"

Not too many years ago, I was walking down the street and saw a beautiful woman. I heard a voice saying, "What a great mommy she would be!" That voice was my inner child! Thank God I am able to tell the difference between my adult self and my inner child. Our inner children can easily lead us astray in our selection of partners if we are not able to tune into our IC's thoughts. Part of our work must be learning how to listen to our IC and not letting our IC control our decisions.

When we adoptees and mothers of adoption loss are not allowed to grieve, do not have any acknowledgment of our pain, anger and sadness, the emotions will seek other outlets. Our inner world is filled with the absence of our other and we have to shut down emotionally to survive. This contributes to what can look like ADD or ADHD. We can lose our basic sense of self. We can lose our ability to experience our emotions. As Kathryn Asper put it in, "The Abandoned Child Within", we may experience ourselves as being in the depths of hell.'

Earlier, I mentioned Free Floating Anger. We adoptees and moms may have Free Floating Sadness. The deep deep pain [Her Absence Filled My World] may show itself by a sudden bout of crying for no apparent reason. The reason is usually the hidden sadness of our loss.

We must acknowledge to ourselves, the enormity of this absence. We must do this in support groups, therapy, chat rooms and journaling. We must find safe ways and places to soul cry about our missing other. Being with enlightened or loving witnesses, those who have had the same experiences, the same losses will help us grieve. We can be validated, comforted with words and perhaps held while we cry. We need to be able to say, scream, yell, "I want my baby!", "I want my mommy" and soul cry as much as and as often as we can until the need subsides. It takes a long time to grieve but it will be a life time of suffering if we do not.

I suggest that you make a grief list... A list of everything you lost or didn't have because you did not grow up with your natural mother. Include everything you can think of. Allow yourself to feel and express both verbally and in writing (journaling) your pain, anger and sadness about each item on the list. If there is someone close to you who can hold you while you cry, all the better. Also it will help if you can hold your IC committee and let them cry about each item as well.

To Summarize

- The inner world of an adoptee or mom is filled with an awareness of the loss of their "other."
- Their inner world is a vacuum of despair that threatens to destroy them.

Exercise

•   Visualize your committee. Remind them that you are them when they are all grown up. Tell them you understand the pain and are doing everything you can to heal. Ask them to tell you things they want you to write in your journal.

Experience of the Moment

•   You might be in touch with the absence of our other. What does that feel like? Imagine giving your committee a group hug to comfort them. How do you feel now?

Chapter 13

Searching

> *"Searching through the city's canyons where*
> *life's an endless stream. Searching through*
> *the open country for some elusive dream.*
> *Searching every window of my mind for a*
> *clearer view, Oh what am I searching for?*
> I wish I knew." - *Bone & Fenton*

From the moment of separation on, throughout our lives, we are searching. Moms are looking for their lost child, and even as babies adoptees are looking for their mom... We may not be aware of it but we are looking for our 'other.'

"Searching through the night, searching for a light. What my future holds I cannot say. Faces dance and stare, for someone who'll care. Someone who will guide me on my way."

From the beginning, the mother child relationship is a perfect one. Nature insures that the mother and child are in sync with each other and need each other. Mother and child are a unit that nature created to be inseparable. Once the separation occurs, we (moms and adoptees) are continually, unconsciously, looking for the perfect missing "other" in ways that are not readily apparent.

"Searching in this frantic world for a love to call my own, Crossing many bridges leading to towns that are unknown, Standing in the wings of life's drama waiting for my cue, Oh what am I searching for? I wish I knew."

We are driving and listening to music and we get the urge to check out another station because the music might be better. We are watching a show on television and start flipping channels for something better. We are in a relationship and are reluctant to make a commitment because someone more suitable may be out there, somewhere. We get invited to a party but wait until the very last minute to commit because something better may come along. These thoughts of something better are usually unconscious, at least until we are aware of them, then we can start to make note of how often and in what ways this process affects us.

"Hopefully I try, reaching for the sky, Questions flash like mirrors in the sun. What scene must I make? Shall I give or take? What's the final score when all is done?"

What it all boils down to is, I believe, the unconscious desire to reconnect with the perfect other that was denied us at the beginning. Our body and our mind want to continue nature's process and we are usually unaware of it.

"Searching through the waves of loneliness on an empty shore. Searching for familiar footprints, I've known and loved before. Hurry now my love and find me and tell me if it's true, that what I've been searching for, always was you!"

What can we do about this? We need to realize that we can't go back and get what we missed. We can only go on from here. There is no perfect mommy now, no perfect child now. If we are lucky enough to have a reunion we can, with work, have something wonderful but it won't, cannot make up for what was lost. Our job is to accept this sad fact, grieve what we have lost and cannot have back, express our anger about it and then explain this to our IC and help our IC cry and express all her feelings. When our IC fully understands that there is no do-over, no going back, then we can stop searching for our fantasy person. We can learn to live in the now and even make commitments.

To Summarize

- We need to stop searching for what we lost.
- To do that, we must find a way to grieve everything we have lost.

Exercise

- Close your eyes and talk to your committee. Explain to them that it is very sad that they lost their "other", and that you know they want back what they lost. Tell them that by letting you help them they can reduce their pain a lot and be able to stop looking for a way to fix the past. Tell them that *you*, the adult, are the perfect one to help them to heal their very painful loss and stop having disappointments with their lives.

Experience of the Moment

- You might be confused and feeling anxiety. You and/or your IC may not like what I have written. I wish we could recapture the perfection of that mother child relationship that we lost, but the fact is that we cannot. When we are able to accept that we can't get it back, we will be able to move forward on our healing journey. Journal your feelings about this disappointment.

Chapter 14

Genetic Attraction

"Whoever loves becomes humble. Those who love have, so to speak, pawned a part of their narcissism." - Sigmund Freud

"I had an intense desire to lean over and suckle. It terrified me." - A 58 year old woman talking about her reunion with her mother.

This taboo subject, often referred to as Genetic Sexual Attraction or Genetic Attraction, is the force that draws those separated by adoption to want to be close to each other, to recapture the love they missed by being separated. For an adoptee, this force is fueled by the fact that the adoptee has never seen anyone who looks like her. I leave out the word "sexual" because I do not believe that is the driving force.

Let's go back to the beginning. When mother and child were separated, nature's process was stopped. The psychological and physiological bonding process that began in the womb was abruptly stopped. The mind and body were not allowed to continue a very necessary part of the mother child symbiotic unit. The mother is left with full breasts, hormones raging, emotions at a peak and ready to nurture. The infant is taken from everything safe (mommy) and put in the arms of strangers who do not look right, smell right or feel right. She gets a substitute to some degree, her mother does not. Both are left incomplete.

At reunion, nature's unfinished process wakes up. The mind and body want to continue where they left off. The adoptee and her mother want to get as close as they can get. They want to hug, and they want that intense one-ness that mother and child can have. They want to snuggle, be next to each other, and bask in that absolute safety and comfort. This closeness can wake up the unfinished closeness that occurs during breast feeding. Breast feeding is sensual for both mother and child. The two adults can find themselves aroused and not understand it. Their inner children can literally take over and the two adults, unaware of what is truly happening to them wind up engaged in sexual activity. This is not a perversion and not about sex. It's about nature wanting to experience what was lost.

When a mother and her infant are not separated there is a normal formation of a taboo. For those separated at the beginning, there is no taboo. Moreover, mothers of adoption loss have it drummed into their heads that they have no children and adoptees are usually made to believe that their only mother is their adoptive mother.

The best way to prevent GA relationships is to be educated, to prepare in advance for reunion, to learn to be aware of our inner child's thoughts and feelings.

If you find yourself in a GA relationship, please get help but be careful who you go to as in most places these relationships are against the law. I do not believe we are responsible for getting into a GA relationship but we are responsible to stop and get help. While I do not believe it's a sign of sexual perversion or psychological illness to get into a GA relationship, I do believe these relationships are truly dangerous for a myriad of reasons and that one must not continue, no matter what.

> ***The Forbidden Love,*** **by Barbara Gonyo is the only book on the subject of which I am aware.**

To Summarize

- At reunion, our mind and body "knowledge" of the interruption of the bonding process can create an effort to continue from where it left off.
- The feelings involved can be surprising and overwhelming.
- Adoptees and moms are told by society that they are not related to each other.

Exercise

- Close your eyes and visualize being with your IC. Tell your IC that sometimes she may have confusing feelings about her "other" and if that happens to tell you as soon as she can.

Experience of the Moment

- This subject may make you understandably uncomfortable. If you have had a GA experience, please do not blame yourself or your "other" but find some qualified professional help.

Chapter 15

Who Said That?

Reunion is like stepping into the past - "I stood still, vision blurring, and in that moment, I heard my heart break. It was a small, clean sound, like the snapping of a flower's stem." - Diana Gabaldon

Regression happens often, even before and after reunion, and we need to learn to listen to what's going on in our head and ask, "Who said that? Is that my adult self or my IC?"

When an adult is having a temper tantrum, she has regressed to a two-year old. The adult self is not consciously present. A two-year old is in charge. When an adult making $30,000 a year walks into a Maserati dealer and buys the car on credit, it is most likely that she has regressed and it's her sixteen-year old self making the purchase. When we expect our partner to make us feel loved, to make us happy, to be fulfilled, it means we are in a regressed state, wanting someone, usually mommy, to take care of us.

We need to learn to listen and ask, "Who said that?" The more inner child work we do, the easier it will be to figure it out.

As parents, the more one nurtures one's child, meets her needs, is consistently loving, the less that child will be demanding. The less we meet the child's needs, the more the child will act out in different ways to demand attention, to get love and to get what she needs.

Our inner children are no different. The more we nurture our IC, meets her needs, are consistently loving, the less our IC will try to take control. The less we meet our IC's needs, the more she will try to take over in different ways to demand attention, to get love, to get what she needs and to be in control.

When people say, "I *know* I should do this but I am going to do *this* anyway", it usually means their IC is taking over. If we really listen, we'll know when what we hear in our heads is not realistic, meaning our IC is saying it. The more IC work we do, the less we'll hear unrealistic things.

Regression at Reunion

As I pointed out in the previous chapter, reunion wakes up an unconscious part of our minds and our bodies... that unconscious part of ourselves that wants to continue nature's process, to continue the bonding experience and have what we lost.

If we are fortunate enough to have a reunion, a few problems exist:

1. We are not the age that we were and so can no longer do what we would have done way back then, at least not in reality. We can symbolically, and with help, heal some of our losses by processing the feelings, letting ourselves grieve and doing the inner child work suggested in this book.

2. Our unconscious mind can take over in a regressed state of which we may very likely not be aware.

The regressed age of the mom is the age she was when she lost her baby. She wants to nurture, take care of, be a mommy to the adoptee and she is likely not consciously aware of this regression. Her regression is mostly static. It stays the same.

The regressed age of the adoptee is usually very dynamic. Her regressed age changes from 2 days old to 7 years, to 2 years, to 15 years, to 2, to 7, to 1, to 8, to 10, in a whirlwind so fast that it can be hard to keep up... and the adoptee has no idea this is going on. And the mom's head is spinning in confusion.

The things the mom and the adoptee say are the key to the regressed age.

Mixed in with this are the effects of the issues in the "Fear of Mommy Love" and "Conflict between Two Moms" appendices. Also, the repressed rage of the adoptee is often unleashed unwittingly at her mom. Mom wants to be close and adoptee pushes away. Adoptee wants to be close and mom takes this as a sign that all is well forever. When things get too close, the adoptee is apt to be terrified and run without knowing the underlying reason.

The beginning of reunion is often described as a honeymoon but as things get closer, the unconscious feelings from the beginning surface and both mom and adoptee can be swamped with the feelings of pain, anger and sadness that can appear to be unmanageable and we can seem to be in an emotional emergency room. We deserve tremendous respect from all those in our lives.

3.   We and our other are at different stages of awareness of our regression, which is common. Be patient. Each of us process things at a different rate. Be respectful of your "others" rate of change. Understand that fear mixes in with processing time by slowing it down. Take care of your IC and try to get your "other" to do the same. Perhaps switch books so that each of you can know what the other has been going through and is going through. Have compassion for the wounds you have each suffered.

4.   Our other is not able to do the work. We need to give them time. If someone is terrified, thinking she will die if she touches these powerful emotions, she cannot just dismiss the terror and face her demons. We must have compassion. We know how terrifying our feelings are so we have an idea of the terror our other is facing.

What we must do, no matter what, is work on our own pain, our own healing, our own "stuff", our own demons. When we do this, we change in many ways and one of these ways is in our ability to communicate. When our ability to communicate changes, we will talk to our other in new ways, ways that may finally help our "other" to take the risk of doing her work. More often than not, our "other" *will* come around and start to do her work.

No matter what, we must be respectful of our own fears, and the fears of our "others" as well.

If a reunited pair get some help and go through the work together, they can symbolically retrieve some of what they lost in a very healing manner. One *can* have a wonderful relationship if one does the work

To Summarize

+ Reunions do not heal
+ Reunions are not necessary to heal
+ Reunions require work
+ Reunions can be wonderful
+ Reunions cause regression
+ Reunions may send us to the Emotional Emergency Room

Exercise

+How old are you feeling right now? Are you aware that you regress from time to time? Can you journal about it? Try to journal what you remember about the last time you regressed.

Experience of the Moment

•   What is going on inside you? Check in with your IC and
     ask her what she is thinking and feeling. See if you can
     judge your current emotional age by what she says. Journal
     about it as completely as is possible.

Chapter 16

Good Grief

"Only eyes washed by tears can see clearly" - Louis Mann"

"Good Grief" - Those two words can express many things including, surprise, horror and sadness. Our sadness, the loss of what to me is a sacred relationship, is rarely dealt with in a way that will promote healing.

In the beginning, when mother and child were separated, each of us experienced the death of the person from whom we were separated. There is no difference in the experience of losing a mother or child to death or adoption. Baby is here, baby is gone. Mommy is here, mommy is gone. We experience that death but what is different is how we are treated if there is a death as opposed to adoption.

If there is a real death, presumably those close to us will say, "I'm sorry your baby died when she was born, you must be sad, let me comfort you", or "I'm sorry your mother died when you were born, you must be sad, let me comfort you." Those words validate and encourage good grieving of this most tragic loss that society acknowledges.

Every mother of adoption loss that I have ever met was told, one way or the other, that she did the noble, selfless thing, and to go on with her life making believe it did not happen. Every adoptee I have ever met was told that she was Special, Chosen or Lucky (which means she is lucky her mother died for her) and then she has to make believe she didn't lose her mother. These scenarios deny loss and deny the need to grieve. To survive the pain, we have to hide from it through denial or repression.

If one has a tooth ache and applies a topical anesthetic to relieve the pain, the decay that causes the toothache continues unnoticed. If we are not allowed to grieve our losses the hidden pain causes emotional decay. The fact is that un-grieved losses paralyze lives. Moreover, the subsequent death of any loved one is unlikely to be grieved in any meaningful way as the fear of the pain of the un-grieved adoption loss is likely to inhibit true grieving.

If we are afraid of the pain of our loss, we are not free; we are enslaved by the hidden emotions of adoption. To be truly happy, have peace and contentment, we must find a way to grieve our adoption losses.

Good Grief of the healing kind involves letting the pain out with those who have experienced the same losses. We need to have validation from those who understand. We need to grieve the loss of the person, the relationship with that person and the special moments we would have had. It is not easy to grieve a relationship that we did not experience but it is possible and necessary. We need to cry until we do not need to cry any more.

We may think, as I used to, that if we start to cry that we will be unable to stop but we will be able to stop. We may think, as I used to, that if we start to cry that our pain will kill us, that we will be annihilated, the fact is that but we will not perish.

Freedom involves Good Grieving. Together we can do this.

Good Grief! What a concept!

To Summarize

- To heal, we must grieve all of our losses.
- We must cry until we don't need to do so any more.
- We deserve the respect of anyone who has suffered a death of a loved one.

Exercise

- Close your eyes and get in touch with your IC. Tell her you love her and give her a hug. If you have done your grieving, tell your IC how proud of her you are. If you have not yet finished your grieving, tell your IC that the two of you will do it together.

Experience of the Moment

- You might be experiencing some sadness thinking about the grieving process. This is normal when we think about past losses, whether we have grieved them or not. Give your IC a hug and tell her you love her and that all is well.

Chapter 17

Graves

"My mother died ... You know, what amazed me the most the next day after her leaving was the fact that the buildings were still in place, the streets were still full of cars running, full of people who were walking, seemingly ignoring that my whole world has just disappeared." - Marc Levy

"When your mother dies, the lights go out." - anon

"The most painful death in all the world is the death of a child. When a child dies, when one child dies... the one that a mother held briefly in her arms-he leaves an empty place in a parent's heart that will never heal." - Thomas H. Kean

"There's no tragedy in life like the death of a child. Things never get back to the way they were." - Dwight D. Eisenhower

Remember that you've already experienced the psychological death of your other when you lost her. When you find a grave at the end of your search or your "other" passes away...

Two of the worst losses in the world are the death of a mother or the death of a child. When someone suffers one of these losses, their grief is understood by others, sanctioned by society and they receive comfort and solace from others.

As discussed earlier in this book, our losses are not recognized by society as a whole and the loss of our "other" needs to be grieved... not an easy thing to do under any circumstances. You've already experienced this death, but what happens when we experience this death again? No other human beings have to experience the death of the same loved one more than once. We have to do it at least three times (In the beginning, at the time of Fracture, and when we do our grief work) and that is more than enough for any one person to have to experience. What happens when we find a grave at the end of our search or we have a reunion and our loved one dies... What happens when we experience this death a fourth time?

When an adoptee finds a grave at end of her search...

You are hit in the face with this horrible knowledge which means feeling the horrible pain of losing her again, another trauma. The trauma of your initial loss rises up and you have to face not only the pain of the death of your mom but the pain of knowing you will never have a reunion. She will never be real to you and you will never get to see or hold or hear or be held by your very own mother, never know what her life was like. To your grief list, you need to add your expectations about reunion, the relationship you hoped for, the things you wanted to do and say and the things you wanted to have and hear. And, to top it off you have to accept that it's over, your search is complete, your hopes and dreams are shattered. Your trauma is magnified beyond anything most people ever have to endure. Your friends and family may not understand, may poo poo it and say, "What are you crying about? You didn't even know her!" Well, you sure did know your mother. You had a relationship with her in the womb at the very least and she's been in your heart ever since, her absence filling your world. Remember that even if you are unaware of it, you were born loving your mother. That's how babies come into the world. I suggest you write a letter to your mom as part of your grieving work. If at all possible, a trip to the grave would be an important part of your grieving. Bring your letter to the grave site and place it in the ground to be with your mom.

No matter what is said, no matter how little comfort we get from others, we need to be aware that the grieving discussed earlier in this book needs to be done on another level. Careful attention and respect must be given to this additional trauma. We need to be patient with ourselves, knowing our grieving process will be longer. More inner child work will be called for and more journaling as well. Most of all we need to be kind to ourselves and nurture and give comfort to our inner children

When a natural mother finds a grave at end of her search...

You are hit in the face with horrible pain, another trauma. The trauma of the initial loss of your child rises up and you have to face not only the pain of the death of your child but the pain of knowing you will never have a reunion, never get to see or hold or talk to your very own child, never know what her life was like. To your grief list, you need to add your expectations about reunion, the relationship you hoped for, the things you wanted to do and say and the things you wanted to hear. And, to top it off you have to accept that it's over, your search is complete, your hopes and dreams are shattered.

Your trauma is magnified beyond anything most people ever have to endure. Your friends and family may not understand, may poo poo it and say, "What are you crying about? You didn't even know her!" Well, you sure did know your child. You had a relationship with her in the womb at the very least and she's been in your heart ever since, her absence filling your world. I suggest you write a letter to your child as part of your grieving work. If at all possible, a trip to the grave would be an important part of your grieving. Bring your letter to the grave site and place it in the ground to be with your child.

No matter what is said, no matter how little comfort we get from others, we need to be aware that the grieving discussed earlier in this book needs to be done on another level. Careful attention and respect must be given to this additional trauma. We need to be patient with ourselves, knowing our grieving process will be longer. More inner child work will be called for and more journaling as well. Most of all we need to be kind to ourselves and nurture and give comfort to our inner children.

When an adoptee's mother dies after they've met...

You are hit in the face with the horrible pain of losing her again, another trauma. The trauma of your initial loss rises up and you have to face not only the pain of the death of your mom the first time, but the pain of knowing it's over. Your mother is dead. You will never see her again, never get to see or hold or hear or be held by your very own mother again. To your grief list, you need to add your expectations for the future, the relationship you've had thus far, the things you wanted to do and say and the things you wanted to have and hear in the future. Your trauma is magnified beyond anything most people ever have to endure. Your friends and family may not understand, may poo poo it and say, "What are you crying about?", "What's the big deal?", "She wasn't really your mother!" Well, she was your mother. You had a relationship with her and she's been in your heart all your life, the absence filling your world until reunion. And now she is gone! Again! You have a right to grieve and be patient with yourself. Give extra time to your committee of inner children. They will need extra time to grieve as well.

As an adoptee, it is important to note that the number of years you were in reunion is likely to be the age of one of your inner children with whom you will need to have extra grief work.

If at all possible, go to the funeral service and go to cemetery. This will be a very important part of your grieving. Unless you are physically stopped, be there! She is your mom. The rituals at funerals services and grave-side are designed to promote grieving. Also, I suggest you write a letter to your mom as part of your grieving work. Bring your letter to the grave site and place it in the ground to stay with your mom.

No matter what is said, no matter how little comfort we get from others, we need to be aware that the grieving discussed earlier in this book needs to be done on another level. Careful attention and respect must be given to this additional trauma. We need to be patient with ourselves, knowing our grieving process will be longer. More inner child work will be called for and more journaling as well. Most of all we need to be kind to ourselves and nurture and give comfort to our inner children.

When a natural mother's child dies after they've met...

You are hit in the face with the horrible pain of losing her again, another trauma. The trauma of your initial loss rises up and you have to face not only the pain of the death of your child the first time, but the pain of knowing it's over. Your child is dead. Every mother's worst nightmare. You will never see her again, never get to see or hold or hear your very own child again. To your grief list, you need to add your expectations for the future, the relationship you've had thus far, the things you wanted to do and say and the things you wanted to have and hear in the future. Your trauma is magnified beyond anything most people ever have to endure. Your friends and family may not understand, may poo poo it and say, "What are you crying about? "What's the big deal?", "She wasn't really your child!" Well, she was your child. You had a relationship with her and she's been in your heart all her life, her absence filling your world until reunion. And now she is gone! Again! You have a right to grieve and be patient with yourself. Give extra time to your committee of inner children. They will need extra time to grieve as well.

If at all possible, go to the funeral service and go to cemetery. This will be a very important part of your grieving. Unless you are physically stopped, be there! She is your child. The rituals at funerals services and grave-side are designed to promote grieving. Also, I suggest you write a letter to your child as part of your grieving work. Bring your letter to the grave site and place it in the ground to stay with your child always.

No matter what is said, no matter how little comfort we get from

96

others, we need to be aware that the grieving discussed earlier in this book needs to be done on another level. Careful attention and respect must be given to this additional trauma. We need to be patient with ourselves, knowing our grieving process will be longer. More inner child work will be called for and more journaling as well. Most of all we need to be kind to ourselves and nurture and give comfort to our inner children.

To Summarize

- Losing our loved ones at the beginning was painful enough, finding a grave or having them die after reunion is, in fact, losing them again and grieving is an absolute must.
- Making a grieving list, painful as it is to do, will help you process your loss.
- Grieving takes time. Be patient with yourself. We need to cry until we don't need to any more. We may be calm for a while, then have the free floating sadness, then calm again. The cycle will flatten out as long as you take care of your IC and let her cry with you holding her and comforting her as often as she needs to.

Exercise

- Close your eyes and hug your inner child and tell her you love her and are so sorry that this happened.
- Hold your younger self and tell her it's ok to cry in your arms. Comfort her while she cries.

Experience of the Moment

- Can you journal your thoughts and feelings about losing your loved one again? Be as explicit and complete as you can be.
X   Hug your IC from time to time while you journal.

Chapter 18

Taking Charge of Your Life

The treatment of those separated by adoption poses special problems for psychotherapists. The differences between adoption related and non-adoption related clients need to be examined, with particular attention paid to the traps therapists are likely to fall into when treating adoptees. The manner in which therapists can develop the special skills needed to establish trust needs to be explored. Specific techniques and therapeutic images that have proven useful in helping clients access and unravel the intertwined ball of repressed feelings must be examined.

We will look at the precipitating incident that brings those separated by adoption to therapy; childhood memories, dealing with the fracture and its result, problems in living an authentic life and changing ego states, and we will look at the parallels in treatment of the adoption affected people with the treatment of abused people.

Therapists also need considerable special knowledge and skills in dealing with clients who are in the process of search and reunion. We will present in depth information on how to prepare and help clients to search for their others, what to expect when clients have a reunion, and how to help clients integrate this new relationship into their lives.

Events in the lives of those separated by adoption such as marriage, pregnancy/the birth of a child, or the death of a loved one frequently trigger the surfacing of emotional conflict around adoption. Since the pain, despair, and rage around adoption have been deeply repressed for decades, these emotions are largely inaccessible and potentially whelming. Thus, most people separated by adoption eventually need help – either in the form of psychotherapy and/or support groups – in examining and dealing with their emotions. Nevertheless, there are many ways in which those separated by adoption can begin the process of healing on their own. We will focus on steps that one can take to minimize the negative effects of adoption on their lives and begin to construct a healed self.

The first step in dealing with any problem is to acknowledge that there *is* a problem. For many of those affected, even considering this possibility is very difficult. Merely thinking about adoption can raise extremely painful and confusing feelings, some of which seem "crazy" or "bizarre" to the adoptee or mom. Commonly held myths about adoption, adoptees and natural mothers and their attitudes, the illegality and/or futility of searching for natural parents, or adoptees, etc., convey the message that "dwelling" on their adoption is useless, thus further discouraging adoptees and moms from rocking the boat. These feelings and myths must be dealt with before adoptees and moms can begin to examine the impact of adoption on their lives. It is easy for a mom or an adoptee to feel "crazy." She may go through a large part of her life thinking thoughts about herself and her differentness that feel too bizarre to say to another human being.

Continuing your life without your "other" may feel schizophrenic. When you exist in a "crazy" situation and no one will validate it, the tendency is to feel that you are crazy. Lacking the details of the true story of her birth and beginnings, the adoptee often feels that she was zapped into existence, fell from outer space or picked out in the baby store. She feels different from non-adopted people but cannot describe how or why. Moms lack information about their child, how and what she is doing, what she looks like or thinks or feels Moms and adoptees are afraid to tell others how they feel for fear of proof of their "craziness." Going to support group meetings and reading and talking to others will help them understand that they are not alone and their thoughts are not crazy, but normal for someone who has had their experience.

Books provide the most accessible and least threatening avenue through which moms and adoptees, their families and helping professionals can begin to explore the impact of adoption on their lives. There is a list of recommended books in the back of this work and it is very advisable to start reading as you start the healing process. The books can be used as a source of information about the adoptee and natural mother experience.

Myths:
- No special knowledge is necessary to treat adoptees and natural mothers in therapy.
- Adoptees and natural moms have no more need for therapy than anyone else.
- If an adoptee or mom does need therapy, it's probably a genetic thing.

Facts:
- Considerable special knowledge is needed to treat adoptees and moms successfully.
- People who suffer severe trauma commonly need therapy.
- Adoptees and natural mothers suffered a severe trauma when they were separated from each other. Therefore, it is likely that they will need some counseling.

What will drive an adoptee or mom to seek therapy? One of the triggers (marriage, pregnancy/birth, death of a loved one, breakup of a relationship) has usually occurred. The adoptee or mom may present herself to the therapist saying, "I guess my adoption experience has affected me, but I don't know how" or "I have had

an experience with adoption but I was told I shouldn't be affected."
The adoptee or mom may not even think adoption has anything to
do with her life. It may take some time for the adoptee or mom to
realize that the effects of the separation at the beginning radiate
through most aspects of her life.

One task for the therapist is to determine why the adoptee or mom
is coming to therapy now. The adoptee or mom may not
consciously know, but if she can figure it out and understand the
feelings and thoughts that precipitated seeking some therapy, it
will help her see the connection to her adoption issues more
clearly. The adoptee or mom may very likely avoid the issues of
adoption.

One trap for professionals is that the adoptee or mom may not raise
adoption as an issue or even disclose it at all. She may disclose it
and then do her best to deny it's an issue. She may then sidestep the
topic at any cost. Keep in mind that the mom or adoptee may well
feel that her life depends on **not** talking about adoption at all and
certainly not feeling the feelings associated with her experience.

At this point, we should again talk about fear of fear. If someone is
afraid of feeling some emotion and they allow themselves to get in
touch with their fear of feeling that emotion, they may experience
to a degree, the very emotion they are trying to avoid. They will
therefore be afraid of their fear. This fear of fear is very common in
people separated by adoption (as well as others) and can make
therapy with those affected very difficult indeed.

Since the adoptee or mom did suffer many "wounds," the period of
time around the fracture and from then on may well be repressed.
Childhood amnesia, is common for trauma survivors, and in my
experience working with adoptees and moms, a great number of
them have lost their memory of large periods of time of their
childhoods or adolescence. Any direct pathway to the pain of the
fracture is likely to be blocked.

The therapist needs to be aware that an adoptee or mom, after disclosing her connection to adoption, is likely to present herself much like someone with a dysfunctional family who can't remember her early life. Here are some of the areas the therapist should explore with her client:

- What was the relationship with her parents like?
- What kind of intimate relationships has she had?
- Does she believe she was/is loveable?
- Does she believe she was evil, deficient or defective?
- Does the adoptee have a good and positive sense of herself?
- Does she drink and if so, how much?

The adoptee/mom may not be able to give truthful answers to the above questions because her real feelings have been repressed to survive. Never forget that the mom or adoptee has suffered the psychological death of her baby/mother and she has probably not been able to verbalize or acknowledge this loss in any way. Her body and unconscious mind remembers this loss and therefore the unresolved grief about this loss should be a primary focal point for her therapy.

It is harder to deal with a psychological death than a real one because the mom or adoptee is aware that her child or natural mother is out there somewhere and the mom or adoptee doesn't know if her "other" is all right or not, alive or dead, happy or sad. Just like someone who is declared missing in action, for the mom or adoptee, her "other" is also missing; MIA... Missing in Adoption. There is no closure. The mom or adoptee's experience of dealing with this psychological death of her "other" is schizophrenic. For the mom or adoptee there is no reality. She was not encouraged to mourn her loss, but to deny it. She is stuck forever at the first stage of mourning, which is denial.

The mom or adoptee understandably wants the pain to disappear. You can never remove the pain of the death of a loved one, but you can learn how to manage the pain and live with it, if you grieve your losses.

Dealing with the fracture and its effects

The Fracture and Society: Neither her relatives, nor society want the adoptee or mom to acknowledge her feelings. To do so would destroy the myth that there is no pain in adoption, that everyone is better off. The adoptee or mom must learn to numb her emotions about her adoption experience so that she may survive the excruciating pain that no one else wants to acknowledge, which would in fact help her heal. The interwoven ball or knot of confusing, painful emotions gets more and more tightly woven, making it harder and harder to function as a whole person.

At the core of the mom or adoptee's emotions is a giant ball of intertwined, indistinguishable feelings. These feelings terrorize her because they are so pervasive and interwoven, making it difficult to separate into individual feelings such as pain, anger and sadness. She may feel like she is experiencing 17 different feelings at the same time and she won't be able to recognize the individual feelings because they are intertwined, and experiencing the feelings all at once is just too much for anyone to handle. She has a great deal of rage and unspeakable fear of repetition of her loss and the subsequent wounds and these feelings go down to her core. The therapist should always be looking for the rage and the fears as they will be woven into the emotional fabric of the adoptee or mom.

Rage and Sadness: The adoptee or mom must at some point accept the rage and sadness at what has happened. The following things all feed the rage and sadness:

- The sense that someone is missing or something is wrong. (Well someone is missing, the most important someone of all. Her child or mother, and what could be more wrong than that?)

- For the adoptee, the conflict between two mothers, which

has been mentioned earlier.

- Looking in a mirror which, for the adoptee, is confusing indeed. Looking at a face that is not "mirrored" by any other face the adoptee is able to see. Somewhere the question awaits... who do I look like? Where did I get those eyes or that nose? And then inevitably, who is she, where is she and the biggest questions of all: did she love me and why did she give me away?

- Dating or getting close to someone puts the mom or adoptee in touch with feelings of impending doom. As a mom or adoptee begins to get close to someone, she begins to feel more and more at risk because she believes, based on her experience of losing her child or mother, that the person she gets close to will ultimately leave. A mom or adoptee tends to follow one of several patterns as a result of the three traumas. Either she avoids intimacy in the first place, never leaves relationships, no matter how bad, or sabotages relationships, thereby giving her control of the ending.

- The adoptee's birthdays have a schizophrenic quality for her and her mom. The adoptee is told to be happy on a day which is the reminder of the "death" of her mother. If she says she is not happy, she will most likely be told that she is indeed happy and be asked, "What's the matter with you, Honey? This is your birthday, a happy day." The adoptee is in a bind, another catch-22, if she does and if she doesn't conform. Reality is gone. She is invalidated again and her grief gets buried deeper. The mom has to pretend her child never existed and spends the day in agony.

- Any perceived rejection or abandonment or anything that hints of separation of any kind, such as failed relationships, reading or watching Bambi, or other fairy tales, going to camp (or for the mom sending a raised child to camp), the first day of school, death, or just seeing other people who look like their families, may trigger rage and despair for the mom or adoptee. Any one of these or similar events can elicit very strong emotions for the mom or adoptee and she react by displaying a strong need to cling to others, push others away or, display both behaviors simultaneously.

The average mom or adoptee won't recognize her anger, pain and sadness or her fear of trauma reactions because it will bring her to the center of her giant ball of intertwined emotions, the emotions of the Fracture.

In terms of her fears being triggered, the average mom or adoptee can "feel" rejected or get triggered by a street lamp. The fear of all of her emotions is so ingrained in her personality that it can show up for no apparent reason. The mom or adoptee finishes a phone conversation, hangs up and something within her psyche says the relationship with the person she was just talking to is over. She feels that somehow she did something wrong and has "blown" the friendship. She might then find an excuse to make a check-back call, just to see what kind of reception she gets, hopefully a good one, to prove to herself that she didn't make a mistake and lose the relationship.

The difficulty with living an authentic life

"If I don't know experience or understand my feelings, how can I feel that I am real?" "How can I live an authentic life if I don't know my own feelings?" "If I don't feel real, is my life a dream?" These are the questions an adoptee or mom may ask herself. The adoptee cannot live an authentic life without being told the facts of her beginnings. The mom cannot live an authentic life without knowing about her lost child. To the average adoptee, everyone else was born but not her. She feels like she was hatched or comes from Mars, perhaps. To the mom, she was made to believe she is not a mom. Since the mom or adoptee is cut off from the feelings of the *fracture*, she cannot be true to herself. She knows not what drives her and basically goes through her life "blind" to what is really going on inside.

One of the major tasks of her therapeutic work, whether in a support group or in therapy, is for the mom or adoptee to get in touch with all of the emotions that drive her; all the hidden feelings she has about herself, and the world. As she starts to be able to do this, she starts to become authentic or real in a way she can never be without this process. She starts to "see" the world and experience it rather than just exist in it. This is very difficult work because the hidden feelings are so powerful. This process must be done carefully and with respect for the fear of the fear of all of those most potent emotions.

Because they suffered the trauma of the separation from their "other", it is very common for moms and adoptees to navigate their lives by walking on a tightrope that they cannot see. As is common with trauma victims, the adoptee or mom often feels like the initial trauma is going to happen again. After all, it happened once so it *will* happen again. To protect herself, she walks the tightrope. But, where does she put her foot next? She thinks and she "knows" she caused the initial disaster, but not how she caused it. She asks herself what she did wrong and how can she avoid doing it again? She must conduct her life in a manner to avoid doing it again. She walks very carefully, always feeling for the tightrope. Living this way, one is always on edge, always hyper-vigilant, always afraid of something going wrong. She is prone to anxiety attacks and general dis-ease. The mom or adoptee might do well to try the anti-panic attack affirmation offered in chapter Two.

The way out of this dilemma is for the mom or adoptee to gradually, intellectually, come to understand that the initial trauma can never happen again. Once this concept is owned by her logically (not always easy to do), inner child work can be used to change this very painful way of living.

At some point, during the healing process, the adoptee or mom may regress back to a very young age and assume a fetal position and actually appear to herself and to her therapist as a young child. As she gets in touch with her inner child's feelings from long ago, her body and mind take on the persona of that age to which she has regressed. She'll act like a baby or young woman and talk (content) like a baby or very young person; her voice may even have a young quality to it. During these times, there is the opportunity to do some intense inner child healing. The inner child work can help the mom or adoptee know and understand that she is lovable and not, as her inner child assumes, at constant risk for suffering a disaster. The work that can be done during these regressions is of great value to her journey to wholeness.

There are many psychological parallels between those separated by adoption and someone who has been sexually, physically or emotionally abused. Simply put, survivors are all the same in many ways. Except for the precipitating event, most survivors have the same difficulties to overcome; the same lack of feeling lovable, frequent feelings of being at risk, free-floating anxiety, difficulty with relationships, etc. The cause is different and the work is different, but the "symptoms" are very similar. Important to keep in mind always is the profound nature of the wound and the respect that must be given to the difficulty of the healing process. All moms and adoptees need to be treated as if they just had an accident and are now in the emergency room. Just as a victim of an automobile accident who is in shock may well deny the need for treatment, so too the adoptee is most often unaware that she is wounded, let alone aware of the depth of the wound. The mom or adoptee needs to approach the healing journey with caution, understanding that she will awaken some powerful and scary emotions. Much can be done to change the way the mom or adoptee is affected today by her tragic experience of losing her "other" long ago, if the work is done slowly, and at a pace that is comfortable for her.

Here are a few ways of approaching the locked closet full of scary emotions:

The mom or adoptee imagines an orange ball. Inside is the

interwoven fabric of emotions, the unspeakable ball of pain from the separation and loss of her "other." All strands of this ball of pain are woven together. Inside the orange, they are safely contained. The orange ball has a small door with a huge padlock, which can only be opened when both therapist and patient are in agreement. The knob of the door is so big that even with the padlock off, a tiny finger pressure will help keep it closed. The therapist explains that the adoptee's emotions are all confused and intertwined, so that it is difficult to understand her feelings. The mom or adoptee removes the padlock but keeps her finger on the door, just in case. Keep a check on how the mom or adoptee is feeling. No strand is so powerful that it cannot be safely examined. The mom or adoptee pulls out a strand of feeling and examines it. She is asked what feeling the strand represents. The therapist explains that every time she does this, it reduces the power of what is left in the orange ball. The therapist reassures the mom or adoptee that she will never pull out or experience anything she can't handle. This helps to put the mom or adoptee in charge of her emotions.

Alternatively, the mom or adoptee imagines a gum ball machine filled with many different colored gum balls. Each color of gum ball represents a different feeling. The gum ball machine is built so that only one gum ball comes down at once. Another cannot come out until the first one is examined. The mom or adoptee proceeds as above, substituting the gum ball for the strands inside the orange.

Doing this work with the gum balls or the orange ball will help the mom or adoptee start to understand that she will not perish or disintegrate if she feels her true feelings. She will be well on her way to taking charge of her own life and she will finally be truly **living**.

To Summarize

- The experience of being separated from her "other" radiates through every aspect of the mother's and the adoptee's life.

- By helping the mom or adoptee experience her feelings and then understand why she feels the way she does, the door opens to changing the way her experience affects her life.

Exercise

- Close your eyes and try to imagine either the gum ball or the orange ball of interwoven emotions. At random, let a gum ball drop into the chute or take a thread of emotion. What emotion does the thread or gum ball represent? Write down in your journal all that you can about the emotions or thoughts generated by the gum ball or thread.

Experience of the Moment

- You might be experiencing a lot of anxiety about now. Taking the gum ball or thread out and examining it can be a very powerful experience. As scary as they might be, these are only feelings. Look around you to see that nothing is happening now. Say that out loud in your head, "Nothing is happening now, it only feels like it, and we're okay." Take a deep breath and say the word, "RELAX" out loud in your head. You should now be feeling better. Please note that while the emotions are very strong, you have indeed survived. The emotions did not hurt you. You just experienced them. Next time you experience them, it will be somewhat easier and less scary.

Chapter 19

Fitting In

"You will not grow if you sit in a beautiful flower garden, but you will grow if you are sick, in pain, experience losses and if you do not put your head in the sand, but take the pain and learn to accept it, not as a curse or punishment but as a gift to you with a very, very specific purpose." - *Elisabeth Kubler-Ross*

At one of my weekly support group meetings, Reverend Mark, an adoptee, asked me what I thought "acceptance" means and how to achieve it.

It made me think of how I was able to find a way to truly fit in.

First, I had to stop thinking of myself as non-human. Just because I had a very different life experience than most people does not mean I am an alien. Just because people do not understand me, does not mean I am a fake. I did a lot of logical thinking and then explained this to my inner child.

As a child, I was put in the wrong movie immediately after my birth. No clue as to the plot or what had transpired before I was in the scene. I had to find a way to adapt to the script laid out by others. As an adult, I was able to see I had choices. Without being in touch with my inner most feelings, I could never know who I truly was or what I truly wanted to do with my life.

So, I went on my mourning journey. I had to cry about everything I had lost. My mother, my relationship with my mother and the special moments I would have had with her. I had to cry about my lost heritage, losing my clan. I had to give up and mourn the magical thinking that one day the nightmare would end and I would be able to start over with my own mother. I had to cry, soul cry actually, until I didn't need to cry anymore. I needed to do this crying with others who understood and who could give me words of comfort, words no one gave me as a child. Crying until one doesn't need to anymore does not mean there is no sadness... it means that the sadness is no long a problem. It's in its proper place with my other life experiences.

I had to learn healthy ways of expressing my rage about all that I had grieved for, all I had lost. I had to express my anger until I didn't need to express it anymore. Expressing anger until one doesn't need to anymore does not mean there is no anger... it means that the anger is no long a problem. It's in its proper place with my other life experiences.

When all this grieving and anger was all dealt with, I could start to let people in, start to feel connected. To do that I had to realize that I could not be abandoned so that even if I let someone in and they left, it would be sad but not an abandonment. The inner child work that allowed me to do this allowed me to feel connected to people which allowed me to start to feel connected to the world and to the human race. When I found out through DNA testing that my natural mother was part Asian, I immediately started to learn and speak Korean and Mandarin, even sign my name in both languages. This gave me a connection to my past, the only truth I know about my beginnings and was the final piece I needed to truly fit in. I needed to belong here on earth with others.

 By doing this grieving, along with the necessary inner child work, I was finally able to enjoy holidays and even my birthday. I came to believe that my mother is with me all the time. I was part

of her body and still am and she is part of my body and therefore part of my life. All of this brings me joy, peace and contentment. Finally I feel whole and at one with life.

One other thing. I came to realize that my strength to face my demons is genetic. The strength to do this work is genetic, our looks, our intelligence, our talents are genetic. All of these blessings are from our natural family. I became proud of my genes and that, too, is part of the healing process and part of fitting in.

Finally, I have come to know that given the horror of losing my mother at birth, an unchangeable fact, I cannot imagine doing anything else with my life than what I've been doing. I'd change the hand I was dealt at the beginning, but I'd not change how I'm playing it!

This process really works if you work it. I pray you do.

To Summarize

- To fit in, I have to accept my life as it is.
- To fit in, I have to accept my life.
- To accept my life, I have to grieve everything I have lost.
- To accept my life, I have to stop wanting what I didn't have.
- To accept my life, I have to embrace all my feelings and realize they can't hurt me.
- To have peace, I have to allow myself to feel my feelings and never stuff them.
- To have peace, I have to allow myself to be me, no matter what.
- To have peace, I have to love myself.

Exercise

- Try to journal your progress in Fitting In. List each item from the summary above and where you are on a scale of 1 to 10 for each one. Add up your total. The closer your score is to 80, the closer you are to peace and contentment. No matter what your score is, be aware that being on this healing journey will get you there! You can't fail if you do not stop your work. Give your IC a high five!

Experience of the Moment

- You may be feeling disappointed that your score is too low. Do not watch the clock on this journey. My score was 0 for a very long time and gradually it started to change. I stopped grading myself and just let myself feel the process as I went along. Now how are you feeling? Did my words help? If not, journal what is going on inside you. Do not despair. This work works if you work it!

Part Two

Appendices

"It may be to late to have a good beginning but it's never too late to have a good ending." - Anon

Appendix A:

The Respect We Never Got

I've looked into your eyes thousands of times and through them into your hearts and I've seen the *pain* and *anguish*. Alone you have had to endure what no human should ever have to endure. Alone, hiding from the world that exiled you. You who have lost your precious child. Your precious child who is Missing in Adoption and for whose loss you receive no respect. I know your pain for it is pain that we have shared together from the beginning. Exquisite pain because it is ours. At least we have that. Now, as to respect...

Without blaming anyone, I suggest we take a look at the respect we never got. To start with, we need to look at the beginning. The beginning was birth and separation for the mother and child. For the adoptive parents, the beginning was the discovery of being infertile or being unable to bring a child into the family any other way.

It was like a big plane crash in a field. All the mothers and babies lying there crying and the rescuers came and carried them off in different directions. When they got to the Emergency Room, they dusted them off, told them they were fine and sent them on their way. The mothers went home and the babies went to new homes. All were told they were fine. The most sacred relationship in the world has now gone up in smoke. They were told that there wasn't any accident, no crash, forget about it, just get on with your lives. The new parents of the babies were told the babies were fine and they should treat all the babies as if they were their own. *As If.* That's a great little phrase. *As If.*

As if is sort of like treating my cat as if she is the German Shepherd dog I really wanted. But I get so frustrated. She won't fetch, she doesn't bark at the door and she won't get my slippers. I love her, but I get so angry she doesn't behave the way I want her to. As if just doesn't work.

So what really happened to each of those mothers and babies from the plane crash? As I see it, there is no substantial difference between the experience of losing a child to death and losing a child to adoption except if there were a real death of a child shortly after birth, the mother's family and friends would have gathered around and said to her I am so sorry your baby died. You must be sad, let me comfort you, I know you hurt, let me ease your pain. I know you must be angry, let me help you. There would be a funeral and grieving and acknowledgment of what really happened, and there would be a grave to go to and there would be validation and healing. This mother would be given respect.

Instead, the mother who loses her child to adoption experiences the psychological death of her child. Instead of comfort, she gets told she did a brave and noble, unselfish, loving thing and she must forget about it, go on with her life. No one wants to help her talk about it, acknowledge it, cry about it, or mourn the loss of her child. So the loss becomes almost unresolvable. The grief stays stuck in her body and unexpressed grief is destructive. She has to go into a kind of shock to survive, hit the pause button on her life and she goes numb. Life is forever changed. You can't really live that way, but you can exist. She gets no respect.

If there were a real death of a mother shortly after birth, at some point, the child's father would tell the child that mommy died and it is so sad that this happened to you and you must hurt, let me comfort you and ease your pain and I know you must be angry, let me help you... and there would be pictures and stories and a grave to visit, and grieving, and eventually the child would find out that mommy didn't die on purpose. This child would be given respect.

Instead for the child whose mother surrenders her to adoption, the child suffers the psychological death of her mother. But she is told that she is special and chosen and lucky. She is supposed to forget that there was another mother. Make believe this is your only family; make believe that all is well. "As if" it is your own. The message is that it is a good thing your mother is not there for you, is dead for you. You are not allowed to be sad about it, acknowledge the pain, anger or sadness, perhaps even to yourself. You are not allowed to mourn the loss of your own mother. The grief gets stuck in your body and unexpressed grief is destructive. (So is keeping in anger and sadness). The child has to go into a kind of shock and go numb. You can't really live that way, but you can pretend. We adoptees are great pretenders. This child gets no respect.

What would happen if your mother died today and you were told you couldn't cry, you couldn't go to the funeral and you had to make believe she never existed. What would happen to you? Take a moment and think about it.

Isn't that what happened to most people in adoption in some way?

It occurs to me that if we really had respect for the mother and the child we would do all we could to preserve the sanctity of that relationship and not separate them at all. If the mother and child could not possibly stay together, then giving her respect when she lost her child, the mother's family and friends would have gathered around and said to her, "I am so sorry you couldn't keep your baby. You must be sad, let me comfort you. I know you hurt, let me ease your pain. I know you must be angry, let me help you." Then there would be grieving and acknowledgment of what really happened.

If the mother and child could not possibly stay together, then giving the adoptee respect when she lost her mother, the new family would say, "You must be sad you lost your natural family, it's okay to cry about it. I'm sad too, you must hurt. Let me comfort you, you must be angry, let me help you, be with you and hold you."

If adoptive parents got respect, they would have gotten complete information on their adopted child and the truth about the effects on their child of losing the natural family. The adoption agency and others would have acknowledged the sadness of infertility or inability to have a child on one's own. Their pain and anger would have been acknowledged and they would have been encouraged to grieve the child they couldn't have on their own.

Ignoring the realities of adoption increases the pain and hurt. How can anyone function well if they're told that what is true isn't and what isn't true is?

For example, what if I lose my leg in an accident right after birth? And they tell me I didn't lose my leg right after I was born, I was mistaken. But it hurts, mommy, and yet it still feels like something is missing. And I keep stumbling around as if I had only one leg (they wouldn't lie about that would they?) and I don't know why I'm having trouble managing as a two-legged person...

Our society doesn't want to acknowledge what has happened to all of us, to give us respect. Truth be told, I lost more than a leg, I lost my mother. Wait, I've got a prosthesis, a new mother, a

"My belief (as an adoptee) is that our mothers are not the objects of our discomfort. What *is* the object of our discomfort is the respect we never got and the grieving and pain of losing our mothers. Our discomfort is in facing the reality of our losses, the truths we didn't have growing up, believing we were unlovable because we weren't kept. Even if the terrible separation occurs, if we are given the respect of truth, of a reunion around age 7 or 8, of photos and stories and the gift of being able to feel our own feelings, we would not push our mothers away." Female adoptee, age 57 substitute. Why doesn't it work just as well? Why does it still hurt? Of course our natural mothers lost a baby... but they got no replacement, no substitute.

Respect is truth, no secrets, absolute honesty. We can all deal with the truth.

Have we in adoption had our eyes wide shut? Isn't it time they were wide open?

Well, how can we give ourselves the respect we never got? By learning to experience our feelings. By learning to make "I" statements about our experience.

By learning to say I feel sad because_____, I feel angry because_____, I hurt because_____ (fill in the blank). When we say these things out loud for the first time and get validated for the first time, our feelings become real in a way they can never be if unexpressed. Once our feelings become real, we can start to understand why we feel what we feel and once we understand why we feel what we feel, we can start to change the way our experience affects us today.

We can respect ourselves by expressing our anger at what happened to us. Having anger about something that happened to us and expressing it does not make us angry people. We need to express it. If we don't talk our anger out, we will surely act it out or act it in, in either case, it is destructive. It is poison and will poison our lives and relationships unless we release it.

We can respect ourselves by expressing our sadness. Feeling sad about something sad that happened does not make us crybabies or wimps. We need to express it. Keeping our pain in is destructive. It is poison and it will poison our lives and our relationships unless we release it.

The only way that I know of to be truly happy is to give ourselves the respect of feeling all of our feelings. If we don't feel the bad ones, we cannot feel the good ones.

Those around us often try to minimize our losses, our experience. We must not buy into that. We can respect ourselves by acknowledging the true extent of the effects on us of the events at the beginning. If we don't acknowledge the full extent of our wounds, we cannot heal. Only by acknowledging the truth can we begin to heal from our wounds. If I am in an accident and go to the ER and they don't examine my wounds, don't clean the depths of my wounds and get the dirt or poison out, I will get an infection, the wound may heal superficially, but the infection is there nevertheless and I will pay a price. Only when I respect myself and take the risk of opening that wound again and cleaning it out will I be able to truly heal.

Healing involves a lot of pain, but the alternative... I guess we have all lived it. We need to give ourselves the respect to climb the mountain of pain that leads to healing. The mountain is steep, but climbable. There are many crevices on the way up, but each crevice still puts you closer to the top. We are all here in this adoptive family to help each other, nurture each other, support each other, share with each other and learn from each other on this road to respect and healing.

Clarissa Pinkola Estés, who wrote *Women Who Run with the Wolves*, has said that those who have been "abandoned" and face it and work it through can become the strongest people on the face of the earth.

Don't doubt it for a second. Only the truly brave do this work, come to conferences and support groups and work it through.

The alternative to doing the work — well, we can continue to bury our heads like an ostrich, but if we do, we will likely get kicked in the behind and not see it coming. Or to put it another way, if we continue to swim in Denial we will likely get bitten by a crocodile.

To Summarize

- All those involved in adoption have suffered large losses.
- It is much healthier to deal with truth.
- Adoptive parents need to grieve their losses before they adopt.

Exercise

- If you are not one of the above, try to put yourself in their shoes and write down what you might feel if you were in their situation.

Experience of the Moment

- You might be feeling confused, scared or sad or all of these emotions. Anyone would likely feel that way. All humans need to be able to feel sad about sad things. As humans, we need to be able to grieve our losses and cry about them, as that is the only way to mourn. It is truly painful to cry, but crying lets the pain out. Keeping the pain and sadness inside is destructive. Letting it out is truly healing.

Appendix B:

Loss in The Adoption Hand-Off
(by Darlene Gerow and inspired by Ken Watson, Ph.D.)

Before we begin, please list your most favorite in each of the five categories.

Write your choices down.

Your most favorite: **Sound**

Your most favorite: **Taste**

Your most favorite: **Smell**

Your most favorite: **Place**

Your most favorite: **Person**

Although difficult, choose among your favorites, discarding the one you will miss least. Continue discarding until all of your favorites are gone.

Take careful note of how it feels to imagine losing all of your most favorites, including your most favorite person.

A child's favorites are perhaps easier to recognize, but please consider the favorites of babies and the very real losses they experience during the hand-off at adoption.

Baby's most favorite **Sound**	The regular in and out of my mother's breathing and the dependable rhythm of her heart beat. But mostly the sound of her voicc.
Baby's most favorite **Taste**	My mother's milk, created exclusively for me. And the taste of her skin, her breast. It is all one.
Baby's most favorite **Smell**	The scent of my mother's skin as I bury my face in her neck. It is basic and right. It is where I belong.
Baby's most favorite **Place**	Cradled in my mother's arms, next to the sounds and smells and tastes that I have experienced since my conception. This is my home.
Baby's most favorite **Person**	My mother is my universe. She is a part of me, just as I am a part of her. No one can replace her. If I am separated from her, I will long for her my entire life.

Adoptees, regardless of their age, whether they are newborn or older, domestically adopted or foreign, give up all of their favorite things when they are adopted.

The loss begins with their name. They lose all information about themselves and their origins. They lose their identity.

They lose it all. They lose the smells and tastes and sounds and places and people with whom they are familiar... all of their favorites. Everything they have ever known is gone and changed forever.

Their greatest loss, which you surely understand, is the loss of their favorite person. Mommy! They lose their most favorite person irrevocably.

If there must be a separation of mother and child, if there is no other way, by recognizing an adoptee's loss, we can endeavor to ease the pain by maintaining as much of her previous life as possible. With empathy we can make their transition more humane.

Author's comments:

There is evidence that a newborn "knows" when she is looking into the eyes of her natural mother or someone else. This may explain the apparent high percentage of vision problems among the adopted population. If the infant does indeed know when she is not looking into her natural mother's eyes, she has lost another of her favorite thing and her general anxiety would be even more pronounced.

"The bond between a mother and her child is naturally sacred. It is physical, psychological and spiritual. It is very resilient and very flexible. It can stretch very far - naturally. Any artificial or violent injury to this 'stretch' constitutes a serious psychic trauma to both mother and child - for all eternity. This means that children need their mothers and mothers need their children - whether or not a mother is married or unmarried." - *Mothers On Trial, The Battle For Children and Custody* - by Phyllis Chesler

A mother's losses from the Adoption Hand-off are the flip side of the adoptee's losses. Just as big, just as important, just as irrevocable, just as painful, just as sad and just as tragic.

To Summarize

- Everything about her mother is baby's favorite.
- The loss of these favorite things is monumental

Exercise

- Close your eyes and try to imagine what it would be like if your newborn baby was kidnapped or you found out that you as a baby were kidnapped. What would go on inside you? What would you feel?

Experience of the Moment

- You might be experiencing some tightness in your chest or some anxiety or pain. Check in with your IC. What can she tell you about her feelings regarding kidnapping. Can you journal your thoughts and feelings?

Appendix C:

Adoptee's Preparation for Search

If one wants to learn how to fly a plane, one takes flying lessons. Ground school first, then flying with an instructor, then when one has enough knowledge to handle anything that happens, one can solo. If one just hops in a plane, without doing the work, one is likely to crash and burn. One might do well, but the odds are against it.

Preparation for reunion is like taking flying lessons. Ground school involves reading adoption related literature. Going to groups, counseling, chat rooms and talking to other adoptees and moms is your flight time. If you just jump in without the prep, you might do ok, but the odds are you will sabotage your reunion.

Reunions cannot and do not fix our pain. Reunions always bring up the pain of our losses which is normal and necessary. The better the reunion, the deeper the pain. The pain of our losses, the pain of what we missed. One must walk through this pain to heal. The rewards of doing this prep work are beyond compare.

From those who have prepared, I have never ever heard, "I wish I had not done this." From those who have not prepared, I often hear, "I wish I had gotten ready before I searched."

"From those who prepared, what I usually hear is, "Thank God I was ready!" I pray you prepare.

You know you are ready to search when:

You have read and understood "The Girls Who Went Away".

You have talked to other moms and adoptees.

You have read and understood "Primal Wound".

You have read, and understood "Adoption Healing... a path to recovery (for Adoptees)" and done all the exercises.

You have read, and understood "Adoption Healing... a path to recovery (for Moms)" and done all the exercises.

You are journaling and channeling your anger daily.

You are talking to your Inner Child daily.

You have done the lovability affirmations and your Inner Child has told you that she/he is and always was lovable.

Your Inner Child has told you about her/his rage at mommy for not being kept.

You have convinced your IC that mommy had no choice, that it was not her fault and that it's not fair to be angry at her.

Your IC has said the above to you.

You and your IC know you cannot get rejected when you make contact.

You have grieved the loss of your mom and the relationship you might have had with her.

You understand that you have an obligation to continue a relationship with your mom if she wishes to do so.

You've read and understood the Reunion Guidelines. (Appendix E)

You've read and understood the Language of Adoption. (on line)

You have written down all the possibilities that you may find and know that no matter what you find, you will be ok.

You have let yourself experience the feelings that would exist for each possibility above.

You have read about genetic attraction and know to be on guard for those feelings so as to not get into a bad situation.

You know that reunions do not fix anything.

To Summarize

- Preparation for search involves a lot of work.
- If you prepare, you will have a win-win situation.
- If you don't prepare, you will be cheating yourself.

Exercise

- Close your eyes and imagine your mother knocks on your door unexpectedly. What goes through your mind?

Experience of the Moment

- Journal your thoughts and feelings about having an unexpected reunion.

Appendix D:

Mother's Preparation for Search

If one wants to learn how to fly a plane, one takes flying lessons. Ground school first, then flying with an instructor, then when one has enough knowledge to handle anything that happens, one can solo. If one just hops in a plane, without doing the work, one is likely to crash and burn. One might do well, but the odds are against it.

Preparation for reunion is like taking flying lessons. Ground school involves reading adoption related literature. Going to groups, counseling, chat rooms, talking to other adoptees and moms is your flight time. If you just jump in without the prep, you might do ok, but the odds are you will sabotage your reunion.

Reunions cannot and do not fix our pain. Reunions always bring up the pain of our losses which is normal and necessary. The better the reunion, the deeper the pain. The pain of our losses, the pain of what we missed. One must walk through this pain to heal. The rewards of doing this prep work are beyond compare.

From those who have prepared, I have never ever heard, "I wish I had not done this." From those who have not prepared, I often hear, "I wish I had gotten ready before I searched." "From those who prepared, what I usually hear is, "Thank God I was ready!" I pray you prepare.

You know you are ready to search when:

You have read and understood "The Girls Who Went Away".

You have talked to other moms and adoptees.

You have read and understood "Primal Wound".

You have read, and understood "Adoption Healing... a path to recovery (for Moms)" and done all the exercises.

You have read, and understood "Adoption Healing... a path to recovery (for Adoptees)" and done all the exercises.

You are journaling and channeling your anger daily.

You are talking to your Inner Child daily.

You have done the lovability affirmations and your Inner Child has told you that she/he is and always was lovable.

Your Inner Child has told you about her/ rage at not being allowed to keep her child.

You have convinced your IC that she had no choice, that it was not her fault. IC has said the above to you.

You and your IC know you cannot get rejected when you make contact.

You have grieved the loss of your child and the relationship you might have had with her.

You've read and understood the Reunion Guidelines. (Appendix E)

You've read and understood the <u>Language of Adoption</u>. (on line)

You understand that you have an obligation to continue a relationship with your child if she wishes to do so.

You have written down all the possibilities that you may find and know that no matter what you find, you will be ok.

You have let yourself experience the feelings that would exist for each possibility above.

You have read about genetic attraction and know to be on guard for those feelings so as to not get into a bad situation.

You know that reunions do not fix anything.

To Summarize

- Preparation for search involves a lot of work.
- If you prepare, you will have a win-win situation.
- If you don't prepare, you will be cheating yourself.

Exercise

- Close your eyes and imagine your lost child knocks on your door unexpectedly. What goes through your mind?

Experience of the Moment

- Journal your thoughts and feelings about having an unexpected reunion.

Appendix E:

Guidelines for Adoption Reunions

These guidelines are not cast in stone! Preparation before contact is a must.
(Refer to the guidelines for preparation in Appendices C & D)

0. Nobody knows the "rules", especially the person who is found.

1. Adoptees may "back off" even if they did the search.

2. Mothers reuniting with their child may not "back off", - especially if they searched.

3. Everyone needs "space", but not endless space.

SPACE means:

> Separation
> Patience
> Acknowledgment
> Concern
> Empathy

4. For those "in space", a simple card signed "Happy Birthday" or "Thinking of You", are acceptable: this can go on for YEARS, so do *not* have "great expectations".

5. SLOW is the pace, especially at the outset.

6. Do not launch into long or angry letters before meeting.

7. Not everything is adoption/reunion related, but separation at birth is a core issue that radiates through almost everything else.

8. Expect that an adoptee will express anger, somehow, some way, probably not overtly, possibly not even recognizing that he or she is angry.

9. When reunion is new, talk to one another about the boundaries you need to establish. (Again, the adoptee has leeway, but the mother must remain in the "responsible adult" role.)

10. Join a support group. Sharing and learning with others is most important. A face to face group is best.

11. Start your own grief work. Seek professional help if needed.

12 Help your current family and friends to understand that search and reunion will be your "life focus" for a while. Share that you may need a supportive shoulder or open ears. "Advice" may not be heard! Remember that your friends may not understand.. Even you may not understand.

13. Search and reunion are as much about YOU as they are about finding someone. Expect to change in many ways. Do not expect or allow a well-meaning family to expect that search will "fix" you.

14. Remember that real life is "messy" , unlike fantasy, which you can bend to suit you. If you aren't ready for "real" and ready to give up fantasies; don't search! And certainly don't make contact!

15. Relatives happen! Relationships take time and work to put into proper perspective. (Remember this when experiencing Genetic Attraction, too!)

16. Family is, ideally, supposed to be fun, thought-provoking, and supportive of each other, while still respectful of independence.

To Summarize

- No one knows the rules for reunion.
- We must be respectful of the feelings of the person found.
- Just because we are ready does not mean they are.

Exercise

- Close your eyes and try to imagine what it would be like to be unprepared to be contacted. Ask your IC what she thinks and feels about it.

Experience of the Moment

- You might be afraid right now or perhaps happy and anxious at the same time. Journal as much as you can about this confusing topic. Spend some special time doing something fun with your Inner Child..

136

Appendix F:

Healing Weekends

"One of the saddest things of all is that so many adoptees and moms are afraid to take the risk of healing which is necessary to pursue one's dreams"

I facilitate healing weekends six times annually. These weekends are for adoptees and mothers of adoption loss. People may attend alone or attend as reunited pairs. The focus is on inner child work along with visualizations and dealing with all the feelings that are difficult to manage.

"The truth that many people never understand, until it is too late, is that the more you try to avoid suffering the more you suffer because smaller and more insignificant things begin to torture you in proportion to your fear of being hurt" - Tomas Merton

As to Healing Weekends:

A quiet country setting... on a private lake...Where understanding, acceptance and empowerment happen for those involved in adoption Two days of healing with adoptees and mothers who have lost children to adoption. (As well as the lovable pussycats in residence.)

*** You do not have to be reunited to attend, except for the paired weekends.

These weekends, for adoptees and mothers who lost children to adoption, are a carefully developed progression of exercises. These exercises lead people to feel safe and enhance visualizations leading to Inner Child work. They will also allow you to explore the ability to experience the feelings that are so scary. As the weekend progresses you will be able to combine these exercises to do some deep healing and learn ways to help yourself come to some inner peace.

For the healing weekend schedule, location & travel information,

Email Adoption Healing: info@adoptionhealing.com

"There is no failure except in no longer trying. There is no defeat except from within, no really insurmountable barrier save our own inherent weakness of purpose." - Elbert Hubbard

Appendix G:

How to Love Your Inner Child

Be there no matter what.

Say, "I love you" as often as possible.

Give hugs as often as possible.

Say Yes as often as possible.

Let her bang on pots and pans.

If she is crabby, tell her you love her and it's okay to be crabby.

If she is doing things she shouldn't, tell her you love her and find fun things to do together.

Realize how important it is to be a child.

Read books out loud with joy.

Invent pleasures together.

Remember how really small she is.

Giggle a lot.

Surprise her.

Say No when necessary.

Teach Feelings.

Heal your Inner Child with love and love and love.

Learn about parenting.

Hug trees together.

Make loving a safe thing.

Bake a cake and eat it with no hands.

Go find elephants and kiss them.

Paint raindrops.

Plan to build a rocket ship.

Imagine yourself as magic.

Make lots of forts with blankets.
Let your angel fly.

Reveal your own dreams.

Search out the positive.

Keep the gleam in your eye.

Mail letters to God.

Encourage silliness.

Plant Licorice in your garden.

Open up.

Stop Yelling. (Forever)

Express your love.

Speak Kindly.

Paint her tennis shoes.

Handle with caring.

Remember that children are miraculous

Appendix H:

Chat Room – Adoptese

(Where we learn *Adoptese*, the language of adoption.)

This chat is for adoptees, their relatives and natural parents and their relatives.

Chat is open 24/7 and is facilitated nightly from 11 pm to 1 am Eastern Standard/Daylight time.

Guidelines - Important - PLEASE READ

We do not use the word "adopter". Adoptive parents may be referred to as "Adoptive Parents" or "A-rents" or "Aparents".

We do not use the words "bio", "biological" or "birth" in reference to our first mothers.

Who you see in chat, what you see in chat, when you leave chat, let it stay in chat, EXCEPT IN EMERGENCIES. If you think there is a possibility that someone in chat may harm themself or others, please let the facilitator know immediately.

Feelings

Basic Feelings are: Mad, Sad, Glad, Fear, Shame, Guilt, Jealousy

Examples of feelings statements:

"I am angry I was not raised by my natural mother."

"I am sad I did not get to raise my child. I'm afraid that I will die if I work on my pain."

Abbreviations

Chat Abbreviations: **brb** = Be Right Back, **lol** = Laughing out Loud, **roflmao** = Rolling On Floor, Laughing My Ass Off, **ic** = Inner Child, **ty** = Thank You, **yw** = You're Welcome, **wb** = Welcome Back

To Join:

If you are not a member, please email joesoll@adoptionhealing.com telling me your connection to adoption and requested screen name, which must include your 1st name. Your password will be emailed back.

Gossip inside and outside of our chat hurts our mission of healing from adoption wounds.

Please keep chat confidential, except in emergencies.

Link for chat: www.adoptionhealing.com/chat.shtml

Links for E-book or Kindle versions of this book.

Code of Conduct: Language
http://www.adoptionhealing.com/language.htm

Adoption Healing Video
http://www.youtube.com/watch?v=5d3tqeuAeME

Adoptee Video
http://www.youtube.com/watch?v=2bIf9tm8GHY

Mom Video
http://www.youtube.com/watch?v=4qD0mYVtxas

Adoption Healing Book Review
http://cchronicle.com/2010/04/adoption-healing-a-book-review/

Appendix I:

The A, B, C's of Searching

Please don't do someone a favor by doing their search as a gift for them.
It's not truly a gift... It may backfire and many people can get hurt.
People need to prepare in advance, no matter what.

Read the two chapters on Preparation for Search.

A. Anything can and usually does happen when you're searching.
If you're not prepared to deal with the truth of your life, you're not
ready to search. Your natural mother could be dead or may not
want to meet you. Chances are she's alive, living a normal life and
is as anxious to meet you as you are to meet her.

B. Natural mothers never forget. Tucked away somewhere is her
memory of you. It reappears on your birthday and on the day she
surrendered you.

C. Cry a lot and laugh a lot during your search. It's healing.

D. Don't expect a reunion to solve all your problems. It won't.
Searching will make you stronger and may answer questions you
may have about yourself, but it will also bring new complications
to your life and possibly new relationships you'll have to deal with.

E. Expect to feel very emotional as your search progresses. It's common to feel a lot of grief - anger, sadness, hopelessness – as you proceed on your search.

F. Feelings mean you're doing your work. If you're not feeling anything, chances are you're running from something. Expect to feel tremendous highs when you uncover new information on your search and tremendous lows when you find yourself up against a wall.

G. Go to meetings, get search help and talk about your experience. It helps to talk to people who are in the same boat as you or who have gone through their own searches.

H. Hold on, you move too fast. Chances are you haven't dealt with the intensity of emotions you may experience on your search. Searching can often seem like a roller-coaster ride. Sometimes by slowing down, and by not being in such a hurry to have all the information at once, the seemingly overwhelming feelings may subside.

I. Inventiveness pays off. You have to be active in your search. Those who stay on the sidelines don't find. Searching doesn't go by the numbers. The more inventive you and your search helper are, the better are your chances of having a successful reunion.

J. Join a search/support group and a chat (like Adoptese). People who search through a group have a better chance of finding and a better chance of a good reunion.

K. Keep good records. Don't throw away anything that might later provide an essential clue.

L. Adoptees should listen to the experience of natural mothers in the group. Chances are you've never met a natural mother--and known it. This is your opportunity to gain some valuable insights into your own natural mother. Chances are she didn't have a choice, not because she didn't love you

M. Meetings. Meetings. Meetings. They provide a safe place to explore your adoption experience and to gain support from others who are going through their own search processes.

N. Nice people tend to have smoother reunions. It's understandable to experience rage at what has happened to you and at your natural mother. Deal with the feelings of rage as much as you can before you approach your natural mother. Chances are you'll get off on a better foot that way.

O. Only the beginning ... Searching is not the end, it's only the beginning

P. People who don't understand are best left out of the search process. Expect to hear some people tell you that you have no right to search for your natural family, that you are being disloyal and ungrateful to your adoptive family and that you will destroy your natural mom's life by revealing her secret. Natural mothers don't die from being contacted. Experience shows that many natural mothers, once they overcome the fear, want very much to meet their sons and daughters. Your adoptive parents won't die when they find out you are searching. It may be painful for them, but it's your right to search and to know the truth of your life.

Q. Quitting won't get you anywhere. Expect to have powerful feelings of wanting to quit your search at times, especially if it becomes lengthy or difficult. You don't have to quit, but sometimes if the emotions become too intense, you might want to slow the pace of your search and come to more meetings as a way of understanding what you're feeling.

R. Rejection is every adoptee's middle name. Read "The 'R' Word" Chapter. Throw out the "R" word. Expect to feel a lot of fears as you search. But you will find yourself growing stronger at every step as you confront these fears. Expect to feel afraid that your natural mother or adoptive family will not be welcoming, but know that the chances are that this won't happen.

S. Sad as it is to accept, adoption is not all it's cracked up to be. Your experience hasn't been perfect, and a lot of things have happened to cause you pain. To believe that your adoption experience has been perfect is to be in denial. By being in denial you are running away from painful feelings about yourself and about your life. Running only makes it worse.

T. Therapists are often useful when you're searching. They can help you deal with the confusing feelings you may experience. Seeing a therapist doesn't mean you're sick. It just means you're trying to take care of your emotional life and to learn more about yourself.

U. Understanding will be a valuable asset when you meet your natural mother. As you go through your search, you are preparing yourself for your reunion. Your natural mother is not. She is probably still in "hiding" and has not a conscious idea that you are searching for her. Occasionally, natural mothers and adoptees do look for each other.

V. Voice your feelings when you go to support group meetings. As hard as it is to share painful feelings, sharing them will help you deal with your emotions.

W. Wounds from adoption take time to heal. Be kind to yourself.

X. Xpect to worry that your natural mother is dead. It goes through everyone's mind. She's probably not dead, but if she is, you may have the opportunity to meet siblings, aunts and uncles, and even your natural father.

Y. You won't die from your feelings. You may feel like you're going to die during your search experience, but unless you walk in front of a runaway truck...

Z. Zzzzzz Zzzzzz Zzzzz. Sleep a lot while you're searching. It's a tiring experience, both physically and emotionally.

Appendix J:

Search Resources

We have referrals to over 470 locations for search and support worldwide.

Click below: http://www.adoptionhealing.com/whereg.shtml then scroll down and Click on the state/country where the birth took place for search help, **then scroll down and click the state/country where you live for a group for support.**

Preparation and going to meetings will be the most important part of your search!

If you are searching, PLEASE, please do NOT rely on registries or bulletin boards to find who you are looking for. Most people complete their searches through the help of a group. The odds of finding who you are looking for in a registry (all of them together) or on a bulletin board are about 9000 to one against. Search Angels (who work for free or a small fee):

http://www.adoptionangelsnetwork.com/
http://www.planangel.org/
http://adoption.about.com/cs/sear2/a/searchlisting.htm
http://groups.yahoo.com/group/SoaringAngels/

If anyone Promises you anything for a fee, or money up front, there is a strong possibility that they are conning you. Run the offer by us and we'll let you know.

Appendix K:

Resources and Readings

Adoption Healing, Inc. is affiliated with 470+ search and support groups, referrals to therapists, attorneys in eight countries and resources for search help worldwide.

For information, call Adoption Healing at 845-268-0283, email us at, info@adoptionhealing.com or write to: 74 Lakewood Drive, Congers, New York, NY 10920. The Adoption Healing web site at: www.AdoptionHealing.com has over 40 pages of information.

Recommended Readings:

Adoption Related:

Allen, Elizabeth Cooper, *Mother, Can You Hear Me?*

Andersen, Robert, *2nd Choice: Growing Up Adopted*
_____, & Tucker, Rhonda, *The Bridge Less Traveled*

Gonyo, Barbara, *The Forbidden Love* - Genetic Attraction

Gravelle, K., & Fischer S., *Where Are My Birthparents? A Guide for Teenage Adoptees.*

Guttman, Jane, *The Gift Wrapped in Sorrow*

Hughes, Ann H., *Soul Connection: A Birthmother's Healing Journey*

Lifton, Betty Jean, *Journey of the Adopted Self*
_____, *Lost and Found*
_____, *To Prison With Love*

Musser, Sandra, *I Would Have Searched Forever*
* _____, *To Prison With Love*

Pavao, Joyce Maguire, *The Family of Adoption*

Robinson, Evelyn, *Adoption and Loss: the hidden grief*

Schaefer, Carol, *The Other Mother*

Solinger, Rickie, *Wake Up Little Susie:*
_____, *Pregnancy and Power*
_____, *Beggars and Choosers*
_____, *The Abortionist*

Soll, Joe & Buterbaugh, Karen W. *Adoption Healing... a path to recovery for mothers who lost children to adoption*

Sorosky, A., Baran, A. & Pannor, R. *The Adoption Triangle. Sealed or Open Records: How They Affect Adoptees, Birthparents and Adoptive Parents*

Taylor, Pat, *Shadow Train: A Journey Between Relinquishment and Reunion*

Verrier, Nancy Newton, *The Primal Wound*
_____, Coming *Home to Self*

Inner Child:

Asper, Kathryn, *Abandoned Child Within: On Losing and Regaining Self-Worth*

Bradshaw, John, *Homecoming. Reclaiming and Championing Your Inner Child*

Ferrucci, Piero, *What We May Be: Techniques for Psychological and Spiritual Growth Through Psychosynthesis*

Miller, Alice, *Drama of The Gifted Child: The Search for the True Self*

Stettbacher, J. Konrad, *Making Sense Out of Suffering*

Whitfield, Charles L., *Healing the Child Within*

General:

Bass, Ellen & Davis, Laura, *The Courage to Heal: Guide for Women Survivors of Sexual Abuse*

Chamberlain, David, *Babies Remember Birth*

Chodorow, Nancy J., *The Reproduction of Mothering*

Edelman, Hope, *Motherless Daughters: The Legacy of Loss*

Estés, Clarissa Pinkola, *Women Who Run With The Wolves*, *The Gift of Story* and *the Faithful Gardner*
Gallagher, Winifred, *I.D.: How Heredity and Experience Make You Who You Are*

Hermann, Judith, *Trauma and Recovery*

McClain, Gary & Adamson, Eve, *The Complete Idiot's Guide to Zen Living*

Neubauer, Peter B. et al., *Nature's Thumbprint: The New Genetics of Personality*

Pearce, Joseph Chilton, *Magical Child*

Sark, *Living Juicy: Daily Morsels for your Creative Soul*

Verny, Thomas, *Secret Life of the Unborn Child*

Appendix L:

THE CHARTER OF ADOPTEE RIGHTS

This Charter was drafted as a tool for use by the Open Records movement in North America. It can be used to lobby human rights agencies, state governments, etc. to pass as part of their human rights codes, to form the basis of open records legislation (AND the right of adoptees to self-determination). May be reprinted on websites, in newsletters, books or other publications. Persuade your state or provincial government to sign this into law!

- CHARTER OF ADOPTEE RIGHTS -

Whereas ARTICLE 1 of the UNIVERSAL DECLARATION OF HUMAN RIGHTS states, "All human beings are born free and equal in dignity and rights."

Whereas ARTICLE 2 of the UNIVERSAL DECLARATION OF HUMAN RIGHTS states, "Everyone is entitled to all the rights and freedoms set forth in this Declaration, without distinction of any kind, such as race, colour, sex, language, religion, political or other opinion, national or social origin, property, birth or other status."

Whereas ARTICLE 3 of the UNIVERSAL DECLARATION OF HUMAN RIGHTS states, "Everyone has the right to life, liberty and the security of person."

Whereas ARTICLE 4 of the UNIVERSAL DECLARATION OF

HUMAN RIGHTS states, "No one shall be held in slavery or servitude; slavery and the slave trade shall be prohibited in all their forms."

Whereas ARTICLE 6 of the UNIVERSAL DECLARATION OF HUMAN RIGHTS states, "Everyone has the right to recognition everywhere as a person before the law."

Whereas ARTICLE 7 of the UNIVERSAL DECLARATION OF HUMAN RIGHTS states, "All are equal before the law and are entitled without any discrimination to equal protection against any discrimination in violation of this Declaration and against any incitement to such discrimination."

Whereas all Citizens - both adopted and non-adopted - are equal before the Law,

WE THE UNDERSIGNED, recognize that,

(1) All persons have the right to know whether or not they have been adopted. Furthermore, no-one has the right to withhold such information from another person.

(2) All persons have the right to an identity, and to know what their identities were at all stages of their lives. Pursuant to this, all adults have the right to obtain and possess all government documents that pertain to their historical, genetic, and legal identities, including:

   a) Their legal names at all times during their lives, both before and after any adoptions have taken place;
   b) Their place and date of birth;
   c) The identities of their natural parents;
   d) The identities of natural siblings, grandparents, and other family members;

e) All birth records pertaining to them; that pertain to times in their lives both before and after any adoptions take place.

(3) As all persons have the right to freedom of association, adults who have been separated from their families through adoption have a right to establish communication with their original families, respecting any contact preference requests made by individual members.

(4) As all persons have the right to liberty and freedom from slavery, all adults have the right to build loving family relationships with any other adult, without being limited by feelings of obligation, guilt, or loyalty.

(5) Just as two consenting adults have the right to form a legally-recognized marital relationship through marriage, thus two consenting adults have the same right to establish a legally-recognized parent/child (filial) relationship with each other through adult adoption.

(6) Just as two consenting adults have the right to dissolve a marital relationship through divorce or annulment, thus adults have the same right to annul any legally-recognized parent/child (filial) relationship they have with a parent, either by birth or adoption.

Appendix M:

Myths & Facts

Myths	Facts
When there is an adoption, everyone wins.	Everyone involved in an adoption has many loses.
Natural parents are just reproduction machines.	Natural parents are human beings just like everyone else.
Natural parents do not care about the babies they surrender to adoption.	Most people surrender a child to adoption because they lack the resources to do otherwise.
Natural parents soon forget the child they gave birth to and go on with their lives.	Natural parents care forever and have great difficulty going on with their lives.

Bonding begins after birth.	Bonding begins before birth.
The infant does not experience her separation from her mother.	The child experiences the separation from her mother.
The infant is not affected by the loss of her original mother.	The pain and anger of the separation are not forgotten.
The adoptive family is the only family the adoptee has ever known.	The adoptee had a real relationship with her natural mom mother that started in-utero.
Telling the adopted child a good' story will eliminate pain.	There is no story that you can tell an adopted child that will eliminate pain.
The adopted child has no idea that anything 'happened' at the beginning of her life.	The discovery of her adoptive status is a conscious confirmation of what is already known to the child.
The child will not understand what you are telling her.	The adopted child will feel sadness and pain at the disclosure.
Adopted children don't think about their Natural mothers.	Adopted children think about their natural mothers *all* the time.
Adopted children have no conflicts about being adopted.	Adopted children have a conflict between two mothers that starts developing, at the very latest, when they discover they are adopted.
Adopted children do not have any particular developmental problems.	Adopted children process their developmental milestones differently than non-adopted children.

If the child looks okay (smiles etc.), the child is okay.	Children quickly learn how to hide their negative feelings if they are not validated. Once the feelings are hidden or re-pressed, an unconscious process, they are un-aware of the existence of such feelings.
The child feels lovable because the parents say so often.	The adopted child is unlikely to really believe she is lovable.
The adopted child is just like every other child.	Adopted children are different. Their mothers effectively died' for them at birth and they are in pain from that loss.
If the child has concerns about adoption, she will voice them.	Children often will not talk about something their parents are afraid to hear about.
Teenagers act like teenagers and adopted adolescents are the same as everybody else.	Adolescent adoptees have their own set of specific problems that are very difficult to deal with unless help/ support is available.
It does not matter if you don't know your roots, your heritage.	If you don't know true heritage, it creates enormous pain/ difficulty, especially during adolescence.
You get your identity from your adoptive parents.	Your identity is tied to your past and your heritage.
If the adoptive parents do a good job, the adoptee will not have trouble trusting others.	Adoptees have difficulty trusting anything in a world that separates them from their first family.

The adoptive parents made up for the loss of the original family.	Nothing can make up for the loss of the adoptee's family.
The adoptee should get a good sense of self from her/his adoptive family.	Since the adoptee believes she was unlovable, it is very difficult for her to have a good sense of self.
If an adoptee looks happy and well adjusted, she is.	Many adoptees who appear happy are just (unconsciously) hiding pain.
If an adoptee decides to seek the truth, she is emotionally unbalanced.	It is normal and healthy for an adoptee to want to know her own truth, her own beginnings.
If an adoptee searches, she is looking to get even or to get rich.	Adoptees search to complete their identity.
Adopting a baby will remove the pain of infertility.	Adoption does not remove the pain of infertility.
Adoptive families are just like any other family and adoptive parenting is just the same.	Adoptive families are indeed different and adoptive parenting is also different.
Women who lose babies to adoption soon forget and go on with their lives. An adopted child doesn't experience the loss of the first family.	Women who lose babies to adoption *never* forget and their loss is unresolvable. Babies *do* experience the loss of their mothers, even when the separation begins at birth.

Babies don't know one mother from another.	Babies are aware of the loss of their natural mothers.
Babies don't suffer the loss of their first mother. Babies are babies and all can be treated alike.	Babies suffer from the loss of their first mother. Babies need special attention and consideration when they have lost their mothers.
If you tell a child that she is special or chosen she will feel good about herself. You shouldn't tell a child she is adopted. If you tell your child that her parents died in a car crash she won't think about them.	Telling a child she is special or chosen or lucky will not ring true and will make her feel worse. An adopted child will always find out/figure out that she is adopted. Telling a child that her parents are dead will not stop her from thinking about them and will causes a tremendous amount of extra pain and guilt for the child.
The adoptee never thinks about her natural parents. There is no need to acknowledge that the natural parents ever existed. No one needs to mention the natural parents in conversation.	The adoptee is thinking about her natural parents often, even if unconsciously. The adoptive parents are also thinking about natural parents often, even if unconsciously. Everyone in the family must openly acknowledge the existence of natural parents.
A child of this age would not be thinking about his/her natural family.	Children of all ages think about their natural family. In general, there is no reason why

162

Joe Soll

A child at this age should never be reunited with her natural family. Leave them alone and they will be fine. Don't open up a can of worms.	a child of this age cannot be reunited. No one can successfully deal with the pain of the loss of a mother alone, particularly a child.
Adopted teens are no different than their non-adopted peers. If the adoptee has problems, it is either non-adoption related or genetic. An adopted person, if they must have a reunion, should wait until they are an adult.	Adopted teens have their own special set of needs that must be respected. Adolescence is the time of identity solidification and for the adoptee is often very painful and confusing. A reunion should preferably take place before puberty.
No special knowledge is necessary to treat adoptees in therapy. Adoptees have no more need for therapy than anyone else	Some special knowledge is needed to treat adoptees successfully. People who suffer severe trauma commonly need therapy.
If an adoptee does need therapy, it's probably a genetic thing.	Adoptees suffered a severe trauma when they were separated from their mothers. Therefore, it is likely that they will need some counseling.
Children don't need to know where they come from.	Every person needs to know the truth of their origins.

163

Having regular contact with the natural family would be confusing and destructive to the adopted child and her family.	Regular contact with the natural family is less confusing than no contact and will reduce many of the pains and problems that face the adopted person as she lives her life.

Appendix N:

Personal Bill of Rights

1. I have the right to ask for what I want.
2. I have the right to say "No", to requests or demands I can't meet.
3. I have the right to express all of my feelings, positive or negative.
4. I have the right to change my mind.
5. I have the right to make mistakes and not have to be perfect.
6. I have the right to follow my own values and standards.
7. I have the right to say "No", to anything when I feel I am not ready, it is unsafe or it violates my values.
8. I have the right to determine my own priorities.
9. I have the right not to be responsible for others' behavior, actions, feelings or problems
10. I have the right to expect honesty from others.
11. I have the right to be angry at someone I love.
12. I have the right to be uniquely myself.
13. I have the right to feel scared and say, "I'm afraid".
14. I have the right to say, "I don't know".
15. I have the right not to give excuses or reasons for my behavior.

16. I have the right to make decisions based on my feelings.

17. I have the right to my own needs for personal space and time.

18. I have the right to be playful and frivolous.

19. I have the right to be healthier than those around me.

20. I have the right to be in a nonabusive environment.

21. I have the right to make friends and be comfortable around people.

22. I have the right to change and grow.

23. I have the right to have my needs and wants respected by others.

24. I have the right to be treated with dignity and respect.

25. I have the right to be happy.

Appendix O:

UN Convention on the Rights of the Child

An Overview of

CONVENTION ON THE RIGHTS OF THE CHILD

Adopted by the General Assembly of the United Nations
on 20 November 1989

Article 2:	All rights apply to all children without exception. It is the State's obligation to protect children from any form of discrimination and to take positive action to promote their rights.
Article 3:	All actions concerning the child shall take full account of his or her best interest.
Article 4:	The State must do all it can to implement the rights contained in the Convention.
Article 7:	The child has the right to a name at birth. The child has the right to acquire a nationality and as far as possible, to know his or her parents and be cared for by them.
Article 8:	The State has an obligation to protect and if necessary, re-establish basic aspects of the child's identity. This includes name, nationality and family ties.

Article 9:	The child has the right to live with his or her parents unless this is deemed to be incompatible with the child's best interest. The child also has the right to maintain contact with both parents if separated from one or both.
Article 10:	Children and their parents have the right to leave any country and to enter their own for purposes of reunion or the maintenance of the child parent relationship.
Article 12:	The child has the right to express his or her opinion freely and to have that opinion taken into account in any matter or procedure affecting the child.
Article 13:	The child has the right to express his or her views, obtain information, and make ideas or information known, regardless of frontiers.

Somalia and the United States have not ratified this Treaty.

Epilogue

My voice teacher told me a story about one of the most famous of all composers whose son used to go to the piano and play "Do Re Mi Fa Sol La Ti" and walk away. His father felt compelled to go to the piano and hit the "Do" key to finish the sequence.

As adoptees and natural mothers, our natural sequence is not finished and we feel a deep seated (the deepest) need to complete it. Truly compelling beyond the comprehension of most people who haven't experienced it, and many who have experienced the absence of the completion, we numb out to avoid the painful knowledge and feelings associated with the loss that created the disruption in the first place. As Jane Guttman so aptly put it, "This deep seated need [often] becomes a blueprint for living."

I have been keenly aware of and have experienced the pain of the loss of my mother since I was four years old. I was constantly aware of it either directly or indirectly when it was pre-conscious, sort of on the "tip of my tongue," but I pushed it away. I had to push it away in order to survive. It felt like I had to make it not be real. So I denied it. I didn't tell my friends or wife. It felt like the pain and sadness would annihilate me, break my heart in two if I let myself experience the pain. I went to therapy but I refused to discuss adoption. I told my therapist that I was adopted by speaking in metaphors. I told my therapist I would leave on the spot if she mentioned the "A" word. I meant it! I had never said the word adoption or written it in any form ever in my life, and never would, but one day, by accident, I found out that the car-crash story I had been told was a lie.

I went to my therapist in a rage. I started to talk about adoption. I ranted and raved and fumed and soul cried. I found out that it was possible to search for my natural mother. My therapist badgered me for nine months, probably not a coincidental amount of time and finally I went to my first support group meeting. I hid outside, waiting for someone "nice" to go into the building. I followed. I met other adopted people. I found out that I was to be referred to as an adoptee or an adopted person or an adopted adult. Not an adopted child. I actually, for the first time in my life, said the word out loud. I said I was adopted. The world didn't end. That day changed my life forever. I started the process of ceasing to be a victim. I started to talk about my feelings about my losses to my therapist. I sobbed, I yelled, I hurt like I had never consciously hurt before or so I thought. Then the memories of my pain from childhood came back, the constant pain that I had had to put up walls to ward off.

One day in therapy, after a long time in therapy, in the middle of my worst pain ever, crying from the bottom of my soul, my shrink said to me, "Joe, you are finally living." I thought she had lost her mind. I'm writhing in pain, thrashing and flailing so to speak and she tells me I'm living! What nerve! But... I finally understood what she

> My personal story is very unusual so please don't let it discourage you from searching. Most people do succeed in their searches. Most people do not have fictitious birth dates and birth places.

meant. I was feeling my real feelings and surviving. They didn't kill me. I accepted my pain, it was a part of me and showed me the path to continue my feeling and healing. I faced my demons. They felt gargantuan in size, prehistoric and breathing fire. However, my shrink with her infinite patience comforted me with words. That had never happened before, being comforted in my pain. The enormity of my loss was finally acknowledged and I felt more and more pain and I felt better and better in between times.

I have been searching for my birth family for almost 30 years and have never been able to find any birth relative. I don't know when or where I was born. A Scorpio fits me well. I haven't given up, but there isn't much to do with no factual information. I have anger about my inability to find my natural mother or some other relative but my anger is tame. I have anger at the circumstances that led my mother to believe she couldn't keep me. I have learned how to channel my anger and it truly works. I channel my anger into my work, helping people, and into many of my physical activities.

I had thought that if I never found my mother or some other relative, that I would not survive, that I could not be happy. Well, that's what I thought, but the process of searching, being in therapy and going to support group

> "Yes, every place I look, at every face I see, she's on my mind; I've gotta find this part of me. I miss her more, more than before, as time goes by. I'll wonder who my mother is until I die."
> – *I Wonder Who My Mother Is?* –
> Gladys Shelley

meetings, which I think is the most important of all, has enabled me to heal enough. Enough so that while I still hurt horribly sometimes, I don't experience my hurt as often as I used to. When it does present itself, I embrace it, let it happen to the utmost and it doesn't last as long at all.

Most important of all, I'm not afraid of my feelings anymore. They are finally bearable. I am **not** afraid of my own feelings. If someone told me twenty years ago that I would ever be able to make that last statement, I wouldn't have believed them. But I am not afraid and I know that if YOU do this work you too can stop being afraid of yourself and your feelings.

True happiness can only come to those who let themselves feel all of their feelings, the good and the bad. Otherwise, what we think of as happiness may well be the absence of the very uncomfortable feelings. Having a reunion doesn't take away the pain and anger and sadness. Only hard work will do that. Reunions are very, very important, of course. However, they are icing on the cake. Even a "bad" reunion has its benefits. At least you "know" your truth, whatever it is. But the process is the most important part... the "Journey of the Adopted Self" is the key to the healing. In twenty five years, I have never met anyone who told me they were sorry they searched. I presume someone must exist who feels that way and that saddens me. Searching *is* truly a win-win situation.

I know that many of you who read this book will be experiencing much pain. Take a moment and count your scars. Be proud of your scars because they are proof of what you have survived.

I hope you understand that there is hope. The pain and anger and sadness are manageable. You, too, can stop being afraid of your own feelings. You really can! How to do that is my gift to you. I sincerely hope that after reading this book you can unwrap it. It is sent with caring from someone who knows how bad it can be and how good it can be too.

"... as we let our own light shine, we unconsciously give other people permission to do the same. As we are liberated from our own fear our own presence automatically liberates others." - Nelson Mandela

"When you turn the corner and you run into yourself,
then you know you have turned all the corners that are left"
- Langston Hughes

172

About the Author

Joe Soll is an adoptee, author, psychotherapist and lecturer internationally recognized as an expert in adoption related issues. He is director and co-founder of **Adoption Healing (formerly Adoption Crossroads)** in New York City, a non-profit organization that helps reunite and gives support to adoptees, natural parents and adoptive parents. **Adoption Healing** is affiliated with more than 475 adoption agencies, mental health institutions and adoption search and support groups in eight countries, representing more than 500,000 individuals whose lives have been affected by adoption. **Adoption Healing** is also dedicated to educating the public about adoption issues, preserving families and reforming current adoption practices.

The director and founder of the **Adoption Counseling Center** in New York City, Mr. Soll was also co-organizer and co-chair of the **New York State Adoption Agency Task Force**; a member of Matilda Cuomo's 1993 **Advisory Council on the "Adoption Option"**; three time conference chair and board member of the **American Adoption Congress**, a former trustee of the **International Soundex Reunion Registry**, and a former advisor to the **Center for Family Connections**. He is a fellow of the **American Orthopsychiatric Association**, the **National Association of Social Workers**, and a former adjunct professor of social work at Fordham University Graduate School of Social Service.

Since 1989, Mr. Soll has organized and coordinated nine international mental health conferences on adoption for mental health professionals and those affected by adoption. He has been an expert witness in court about adoption related issues and has lectured widely at adoption agencies, social work schools, mental health facilities and mental health conferences in the U.S. and Canada.

Mr. Soll has appeared on radio and television more than 300 times, given more than 150 lectures on adoption related issues and has been featured or quoted in more than three dozen newspapers, books and magazines. In 1994 he was portrayed as a therapist in a NBC made-for-TV movie about adoption,. He played himself in the HBO original movie *Reno Finds Her Mom*. He was featured in the 2001 Telly Award winning Global Japan documentary, "Adoption Therapist: Joe Soll." He has recently been featured in the documentary, "Blood Lines" and profiled in the International Museum of Women. His own story as an adoptee has been presented more than three dozen times on Unsolved Mysteries. He has walked the 250 miles from New York City to Washington, D.C. six times to create public awareness of the need for adoption reform. He resides in Congers, NY and maintains an office in New York City.

My Books

Prior to 1993 when I started my 1st book, I never considered writing a book, let alone six. (The four listed here plus this book itself plus one more mystery that is in progress.

I was pushed, wheedled and cajoled by friends and colleagues until I gave in. I was in my own way. I didn't think I could write a book, so, I couldn't write a book. Once I decided I truly wanted to write a book, I 1 had a conversation with my Inner Child and suggested we try, and if it didn't work, then... it didn't work. He liked that and so the original *Adoption Healing*, started in 1993, was born in 2000.

A few years later Karen Buterbaugh Wilson and I decided to write an *Adoption Healing* version for moms. We had never met so we wrote the mom version by talking and emailing. A rather different way to co-author a book. We never met until after it was published in 2003

A few years after that, Lori Paris emailed me from California asking for ideas to help her promote her first book, "Follow Your Heart" and I offered some suggestions. I had always been fascinated with mysteries, my character being Travis McGee, created by my favorite author. the late John D. MacDonald, .I asked Lori if she had ever considered writing a mystery. She was all for it, so we started writing *Evil Exchange*. We wrote it by talking and emailing. We never met until my 2010 adoption conference, after *Fatal Flight*, our second mystery, was published.

Writing the books was not about money, it was about writing the books. My purpose in writing the *Adoption Healing* books was to educate and help those in pain. My purpose in writing the mysteries was to have fun. I thoroughly enjoyed writing all four of them, especially the collaboration with my two co-authors.

My message to you is, if you want to write a book, write it. Do not worry about anything else. Just write it. You will know you have written a book and you will be proud of it.

Adoption Healing... a path to recovery (2000)

Some books are so good that you can even forgive your friend for "borrowing" your copy and never giving it back. Adoption Healing ... a path to recovery by Joe Soll is one such book.

Adoption Healing, a self-help book, has been passed around among the adult internationally adopted Koreans who have returned to South Korea, and who indeed rely on self-help while living in a country where gaining access to services in their own languages is difficult.

This book is the gift that "lifers" give to one another after the initial fun of having returned to Korea wears off and we are left with the hangover of too many late nights in Seoul's student and foreigner districts, too many ruined intimate relationships or none at all, limited employment opportunities, and the mix of hope and despair that comes from living in a country where we are no longer recognizable to Koreans as Korean.

Our foreign mannerisms, shattered tongues, and imagined histories have been known to elicit pity and shame from South Koreans. How we are portrayed and perceived, and how we want to be portrayed and perceived, therefore, becomes a heated topic of conversation. How must we appear in order to get what we need — whether recognition from the South Korean government, acceptance in society, or more personally fulfilling reunions?

177

Should we try to appear "successful" and "well-adjusted" or even "angry and ungrateful"?

These kinds of one-sided false selves have their roots in the adoptee's understandable fear of abandonment, Soll tells us as he gently guides us into living more "authentic" lives. He explains that adoptees' inner worlds are shaped by mixed messages that force them "to choose between the socially unacceptable reality they experience and a distorted, but socially sanctioned, interpretation of their reality as determined by others." "This book," he writes, "is about the realities of adoption and the realities of the inner world of the adopted person."

Hope for Individual Change

Soll — a licensed social worker, psychotherapist, and American domestic adoptee — simply and concretely describes the adoptee's inner world in 26 concise chapters. In each chapter, he gives examples of "Myths" and "Facts" about adoption, a summary of the information in the chapter, an exercise to write or do mentally, and a grounding "Experience of the Moment" designed to be read after the exercise. Always with the whole "triad" of adoptee, natural parents, and adoptive parents in mind, Soll ends the book with appendices that include lists of "What Adoptees Do Not Wish to Hear" and "What Natural Parents Do Not Wish to Hear," and "What Adoptive Parents Do Not Wish to Hear."

Readers of Nancy Newton Verrier's, The Primal Wound: Understanding the Adopted Child will be familiar with some of Soll's fundamental beliefs about adoption, beginning with, "The mother-child relationship is sacred and the separation of the mother and child is a tragedy for both." Soll considers this "primal wound" to be the first trauma. He considers the second trauma to be the verbal acknowledgment to the adoptee that she is adopted. (It's likely that many transracially and internationally placed adoptees, older adoptees, and children adopted into families where there were older siblings present, did not need to be told by their adoptive parents that they were adopted.) He considers "fracturing" to be the third trauma.

Fracturing is an acronym for the simultaneous feelings that the adopted child is surrounded by: Frustration, Rage, Anxiety, Confusion, Terror, Unrest, Regret, Inhuman, Neglected, Grief.

Fracturing occurs at the "age of cognition," usually around six to eight years old. At that time, adoptees are able to start thinking about their own adoptions. They do so in the face of conflicting messages, for instance, "Happy birthday! / This is the day you were surrendered." Faced with unresolvable messages that cannot be integrated into her reality, the adopted child will resort to her own logic about her abandonment. If not validated, the child represses horribly painful emotions, after which she is actually unaware of such emotions and suffers a "psychological death."

"It is much healthier to deal with truth," writes Soll, and indeed he puts every painful card out on the table: "It's normal for adoptees to be in crisis during adolescence." Adoptees, because of not knowing their origins, finds it difficult to imagine themselves getting older. They have more difficulty maintaining healthy intimate relationships. They have a harder time than non-adopted people finding careers that suit them. "Many people who appear happy are just (unconsciously) hiding pain." He likens the material in his book to an emotional root canal – painful, but necessary.

"I am not happy about what I have written here, but it needed to be written" writes Soll, but, "it needs to be recognized as knowledge that can help heal those already hurt and help prevent some of the hurt for those who may become involved in or impacted by adoption."

As a self-help book, Soll's description of adoptees' inner worlds, while not exactly feel-good material, gives adoptees and the people who care about them a lot to consider and reflect upon. I was personally surprised by the power of Soll's simple affirmations and visualization exercises. Like another reader, I found them to be a little weird at first, but I soon realized that they are very worthwhile. One exercise I particularly liked is this:

Light a candle and then let the flame represent the burning desire to have something that doesn't exist anymore, like wanting to go back and this time be raised by your natural mother. When you are ready to stop wanting something that is impossible to happen, blow out the flame that holds you back from living your life, that burns you with a desire for the impossible.

Hope for Systemic Change

The book offers help like this on an individual level, and also suggests systemic changes in the practice of adoption. To start with, all members of the "triad" suffer huge losses — whether infertility, the loss of a child, or the loss of the mother — and these losses should be truthfully addressed instead of whitewashed with either platitudes ("You were chosen.") or completely denied ("Get over it."). As far as specific recommendations on policy, Soll includes the following:

1. Every effort should be made to keep children with their birth families, followed by the extended family.

2. All adoptions should be "open," meaning regular visits should be held with the natural mother throughout childhood and adolescence, even if the visits have to be supervised.

3. Children should keep their names and heritage.

4. Adoptees should have periodic psychological development "checkups."

In short, Soll is a big fan of speaking the truth and dealing with reality. He is completely in the camp of open records. "A reunion should preferably take place before puberty," writes Soll, saying that a reunion between the ages of six and eight can help prevent the "fracture" and even bring adopted children closer to their adoptive parents. He sees closed records as a symptom of the lack of respect for adoptees, natural parents, and adoptive parents.

Implications for International Adoption

Soll's work seems to be mainly addressed to American domestic adoptees, but it also has huge implications for the system of international adoption, considering that many adoptive parents choose international adoption over domestic adoption for the very reason that they do not want to have contact with a natural mother. Natural mothers of international adoptees are at the time of this writing almost hopelessly separated from their children by geographic distance and hidden paperwork. If adoption agencies took Soll's advice to heart — keeping adoption records open and reuniting adoptees with their natural mothers for regular visits in childhood, for the benefit of the child — would there be so many international adoptions?

What Soll proposes to be necessary for a healthy adoption culture would make international adoption even more dreadfully expensive and inconvenient for adoptive parents. If all members of the triad were guaranteed contact, agencies would be forced to give accurate social histories of children. Honesty would be enforced. Perpetrators would be caught. Governments would have to freely give out visas to non-white people, often impoverished, from non-Western countries or countries of the global south. People would have to see natural mothers as real people — not whores or saintly human gift-givers. Natural parents might get to speak, and the literature on international adoption would have to include their voices. Adoption agencies would have to find a way to help bridge differences of language and culture in ways that are personally meaningful, instead of encouraging adoptees to relate to their cultures of origin as tourists and consumers.

The financial cost for international adoption agencies to heed Soll's advice is incredibly high and may even be destructive to the system of mass international adoption itself. But the human cost of not heeding his advice is even higher. It is simply the reality of today, reflected in the high rates of suicide, incarceration, and mental illness amongst adoptees, as well as "disrupted" adoptions.

Additional Challenges for International and Transracial Adoptees

Soll, however, does not specifically address the additional challenges that internationally and transracially adopted people face, including racialized violence in their adoptive countries and the language barrier if they are reunited. Many internationally adopted people, who as of now have little hope of reunion with their natural families, may be reunited instead with their original countries and culture. (The "mother country" is routinely proffered to adopted Koreans as a substitute for the actual mother.)

Yet we also need a way to cope with feelings of abandonment by entire countries, governments, and cultures. Extending Soll's ideas about individual reunions between mother and child to social groups, it's possible to guess that what is behind the drive by some adoptee groups to represent themselves as purely "Successful!" to the Korean public is actually the fear of a second abandonment — not by a mother — but a country. If they could see who we really are, in all our complexity, would they still love us?

In the midst of so many internationally and transracially adopted people of color checking the "white" box on U.S. demographic forms — lying to themselves and creating a false self for the world to see — adoption agencies should seriously consider whether they are helping adoptees lead "authentic lives." When the adoptee is denied the opportunity to lead an authentic life because of enforced secrecy and lies, it impoverishes not only the adoptee, but also the natural mother and the adoptive parents.

Reality and Recovery

In The Will to Change, *Bell Hooks* summed up why people impacted by adoption need to heed Joe Soll's advice — no matter how uncomfortable, inconvenient, or expensive: "Anyone who has a false self must be dishonest. People who learn to lie to themselves and others cannot love because they are crippled in their capacity to tell the truth and therefore unable to trust."

Adoptees' lives, emotional health, and even our ability to love our parents are entangled with the very policies and conditions that created us. What have those conditions been? Overwhelmingly, those conditions have been filled with lies – our own lies, family lies, agency lies, government lies.

For those adoptees working to make positive changes in these very adoption policies that shaped our lives, it is essential to tell the truth, both personally and politically, to ourselves and to our loved ones. For all adoptees, it is important to acknowledge our complex realities so we can live in a joyful way, so that we can make conscious decisions and, as Soll says, fully experience the world, not just exist in it. Joe Soll offers us paths that we may explore on our journey toward healing, health, recovery, and love.

This is an important book for adoptees, adoptees' partners and close friends, natural parents, and adoptive parents. Soll's straightforward approach and clear organization makes it possible to do the emotional work without being burdened by a text that is too long or laden with jargon. Parts not of interest can be easily skipped over and returned to later. An added bonus of this book is that the writing is simple enough to be understood by people who speak English as a foreign language.

Although it has been nine years since it was first published, Adoption Healing deserves continued and widespread recognition. After all, as librarians say, "Every book is a new book until you have read it." May you enjoy your copy, and pass it on.

Adoption Healing... a path to recovery for mothers who lost children to adoption (2003)

"This book is a 'must read' for every mother who lost her precious infant to adoption. It is the wake-up call for mothers who have 'sleep-walked' through their lives from the moment their babies were taken for adoption and given to 'worthier' people. It will lead her safely through the quagmire of painful, suppressed memory, out of the darkness of denied love, of exile, and into the light of a life fully lived. It is essential reading for therapists. It will equip them to assist mothers into recovery and

beyond. It provides therapeutic possibilities for mothers, and educational possibilities for therapists, to help both understand the depth of the life-long dysfunction in mothers following adoption. There is a long and painful recovery ahead for every mother. This book will help therapists to understand....how deep the trauma goes. This book validates the mother's adoption loss and deals with her wounds. Out of the lies surrounding adoption, comes this truth. How terrible it is to lose a child. No one who reads this book will be able to view adoption as a viable 'solution' to unplanned pregnancy, ever again. This book shows the mother of adoption loss how to deal with the pain and how to reclaim her motherhood and her humanity. It will lead her safely home to herself." - Joss Shawyer, author of **Death by Adoption**

Evil Exchange   (2007)

"**Evil Exchange** by Lori Paris & Joe Soll, a gripping, deliciously readable novel, combines for the reader, the escapism of a true crime/suspense narrative – with the virtue of having experienced a vigorous, moral work-out. The theme is adoption, and the ripples of trauma that engulf families when an adoptee decides to search; and the main characters, painted with great care, navigate a common hidden darkness... that at the heart of every adoption reside issues of abandonment, loss, emptiness and guilt. Using the format of a lively, entertaining novel, with a large cast of characters; Paris & Soll explore the minefield of family life, depicting how emotional time-bombs can, and often do, explode beneath a well-ordered surface. **Evil Exchange** is a *must* read socially meaningful novel, that sheds light on a complex subject, from multiple perspectives." - David Kirschner, PhD., Psychoanalyst, author of ADOPTION: Uncharted Waters... A Psychologist's Case Studies... Clinical & Forensic Issues.

Fatal Flight   (2010)

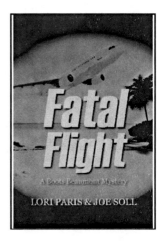

"Fasten your seat belts and get comfortable! **Fatal Flight** takes off quickly and you won't want to put it down until it lands. It was a nonstop flight for me as I read cover to cover in one sitting. I was hooked after the first few pages. The authors open with a bang then use an assortment of interesting characters interwoven through two story lines that eventually converge and lead to a solid ending.

This novel takes the current issue of our safety when we travel by air and gives us a frightening look into what the possibilities are for true evil. If you're looking for a book with a complex and violent plot, yet rich in character detail with moments of humor thrown in, here it is. Fatal Flight is hard to put down.

Timely, clever and masterfully written, Fatal Flight will take you for a trip deep into the psyches of the diabolical bad guys and the detective and his buddies who are tasked with solving this evil plot. Fatal Flight weaves a tale of factual events with the people who might have been caught up in the tragedy and intrigue of this powerful and provocative story." – Avid reader in Washington State

CPSIA information can be obtained at www.ICGtesting.com
Printed in the USA
LVOW040446300612

288325LV00002B/128/P